65 Ways
to Give
Evangelistic
Invitations

65 Ways to Give Evangelistic Invitations

by
Faris D. Whitesell

**Foreword by
Robert G. Lee**

KREGEL PUBLICATIONS
Grand Rapids, Michigan 49501

65 *Ways to Give Evangelistic Invitations* by Faris D. Whitesell. Published in 1984 by Kregel Publications, a division of Kregel, Inc. All rights reserved.

Library of Congress Cataloging in Publication Data

Whitesell, Faris D., 1895-1984
   65 Ways to Give Evangelistic Invitations.

   Reprint. Originally published: Sixty-five ways to give evangelistic invitations. 3rd ed. Grand Rapids, Mich.: Zondervan Pub. House, c1945.
   Includes indexes.
   1. Evangelistic invitations. I. Title. II. Title: Sixty-five ways to give evangelistic invitations.
BV3793.W448 1984   269´.2   84-11269
ISBN 0-8254-4021-1

3 4 5 6 7 Printing/Year 90 89 88 87 86

Printed in the United States of America

CONTENTS

FOREWORD

WITHOUT claiming to be the final word in the matter discussed, without walking with the presumptuous step of a know-it-all, without thinking of himself and of what he has written more highly than he ought to think, but with real humility and with the noble purpose to help evangelistic preachers and pastors to draw the net effectively, Dr. F. D. Whitesell has written a most helpful book entitled *Sixty-Five Ways to Give Evangelistic Invitations.*

There is no dullness in any line of this fine book. Many preachers, as they themselves acknowledge, are weak and sometimes ineffective in giving invitations to the unsaved to accept Christ. To them, as well as to all preachers already skillful in giving invitations, this book will be of great worth. This book leaves no doubt as to the Scriptural sanction of invitations. This book, sensible in the suggestions made and sometimes a bit startling in citing how some have given invitations, urges reliance upon the Holy Spirit in all invitations given and all methods used. It should be read and studied by all who ever have occasion or seek opportunities to "take orders" after setting forth the value of the "Gospel goods."

Put into practice by those who try to fish successfully for men, this book will give courage to the timid, skill to the awkward, prompting to the perplexed, help to the hesitant and effectiveness to the ineffective in the matter of giving Gospel invitations. It is wise, too, in its counsel to Christians as to their conduct while the invitation to the unsaved is given.

I commend this book to every preacher who gives an invitation to the unsaved. It deserves a wide sale and reading and practice.

ROBERT G. LEE, D.D., LL.D., LITT.D.

PREFACE

THE evangelistic invitation is of paramount importance, according to the testimony of nearly all leaders in the evangelistic field. In spite of this sentiment, very little has been written on this particular phase of evangelism. There are many excellent books on evangelism, but very few of them touch on the subject of invitations. I have not been able to find a single book devoted exclusively to this topic. Those few books mentioning the subject either give it a few paragraphs, or a few pages, or at most a chapter. My purpose in writing this book, then, is to fill a gap in the field of evangelistic literature. If this book can stimulate some preachers to give more and better evangelistic invitations, and thus win more souls to Christ, my deepest underlying purpose will be accomplished.

The major emphasis of this book is on methods or techniques, but I have tried to show that these alone are not enough. The work of soul-winning requires much faith and prayer, and entire dependence upon the Holy Spirit and the Word of God. This book, then, is not intended to be a bag of tricks by which the unscrupulous can report larger numbers of decisions; it is rather a compilation of suggestions for those whose burden for souls is so great that they must win every lost person possible.

I am deeply grateful to a number of friends who have given me valuable suggestions which I have in-

corporated in this book. I have derived help also from
several books, as indicated. I am especially indebted
to my colleague, Dr. Carl F. H. Henry, for suggesting
that I write this book. He has also given me valuable
technical suggestions in preparing the manuscript.

FARIS D. WHITESELL

1

WHY GIVE INVITATIONS?

EVANGELISTIC preaching naturally culminates in an invitation. The whole drive of such preaching reaches a logical climax in the appeal. Without the invitation the evangelistic message is incomplete and the effect of the message unknown. An evangelistic invitation is an appeal to make a public response to the claims of Christ. Such an appeal is the most exalted form of persuasion. More spiritual energy and compassion are needed in the invitation than in any other part of the evangelistic service. Invitations are consonant with the genius of the Gospel, and must be given if we are to witness the life-changing potentialities of the Gospel of Christ. The preacher does not fully deliver the burden of his soul until he has given the invitation. The evangel of God's redeeming love deserves an immediate and whole-hearted response, and the invitation calls upon men to make that response in some public manner.

1. INVITATIONS ARE BIBLICAL

The Bible is full of appeals, exhortations, entreaties, pleadings and even commands to hear and heed the calls of God to men. From Jehovah's entreating question to Adam, "Where art thou?" in the third chapter

11

of Genesis, to the final appeal of the Spirit and the bride in Revelation 22:17, the Bible is one re-echoing invitation to lost humanity to turn to Him who came to seek and to save that which was lost.

True enough, we do not find an exact example of the modern evangelistic invitation in the Scriptures, but this fact does not condemn it as unscriptural. Many Christian practices and institutions now in use are not mentioned in the Scriptures, yet we do not consider them unscriptural. We find no references in the Bible to Sunday schools, young people's societies, women's missionary organizations, church buildings, ushers, hymn-books, offering envelopes, church bulletins, communion cards, church pews and the like, but who would cast them all aside for this reason? Anything that helps us to carry out the principles and teachings of the Scriptures in a more effective and practical way is Scriptural. The evangelistic invitation does exactly that: it is a practical aid in bringing men to Christ openly and publicly, and that work, according to the New Testament, is the main business of Christians.

Let us examine the Scriptures somewhat on this subject. Close parallels to modern evangelistic invitations can be found in some Bible passages. Moses gave an invitation in Exodus 32:26, when, after the destruction of the golden calf, he stood in the gate of the camp, and said, "Who is on the Lord's side? let him come unto me." All of the sons of Levi gathered unto Moses, but the people of the other tribes refused to stand with the Lord's people. An evangelistic invitation is designed to call men to take the Lord's side and forsake the world's side.

Joshua appealed to Israel to make a definite decision

and commitment, when, near the close of his life, he gathered all the tribes to Shechem, and said, "Choose you this day whom ye will serve; whether the gods which your fathers served that were on the other side of the flood, or the gods of the Amorites, in whose land ye dwell: but as for me and my house, we will serve the Lord" (Joshua 24:15). When the people said they would choose and serve the Lord, Joshua put it down in writing and had a great stone set up there under an oak as a witness to their decision. Joshua called for a public declaration of loyalty to Jehovah, and had it recorded and memorialized so they could never forget. King Josiah gave a public invitation, when he called an assembly of the people, after the book of the law had been found and read to them, and called upon them to stand in assent to a covenant to keep the law of God (II Chronicles 34:30-32). Ezra called upon the people to swear publicly to carry out his reformations (Ezra 10:5). A similar event is recorded in Nehemiah, chapters 10 and 11. Here a covenant of loyalty to the Lord and His law was made and signed by the Jewish leaders and the rest of the people (Nehemiah 9:38; 10:29).

Jesus gave invitations. He said to Peter and Andrew, "Follow me, and I will make you fishers of men" (Matthew 4:19). He said to Matthew, "Follow me." And he arose, and followed Him (Matthew 9:9). These invitations clearly imply a call for action. It could also be possible that He had some kind of public commitment in mind when He said, "Come unto me, all ye that labour and are heavy laden, and I will give you rest. Take my yoke upon you, and learn of me; for I am meek and lowly in heart: and ye shall find rest unto your souls. For my yoke is easy, and my burden is light"

(Matthew 11:28-30). Jesus invited Zacchaeus down out of the tree, when He said, "Zacchaeus, make haste, and come down; for to day I must abide at thy house" (Luke 19:5).

Jesus gave the parable of the slighted dinner invitation, when the lord said to his servants, "Go out into the highways and hedges, and compel them to come in, that my house may be filled" (Luke 14:23). The American Standard Version says "constrain" instead of "compel," but either word implies strong persuasion. The fifteenth chapter of Luke tells of the shepherd seeking his lost sheep until he found it, and of the woman lighting a candle and diligently searching the house until she had found the lost coin. Jesus did not use any high-pressure methods, however. He was more interested in quality of discipleship than He was in quantity of disciples. But we live in the age of the Holy Spirit, when we are able to do what even Jesus could not do. We must seek for both quality and quantity. We should reach all we can in all the ways we can.

The apostles often used persuasion of an intense degree. On the day of Pentecost, Acts 2:40 tells us that Peter, "With many other words did . . . testify and exhort, saying, Save yourselves from this untoward generation." These words imply strong persuasion. In the house of Cornelius, Peter even commanded people to be baptized. Acts 10:48 reads, "And he commanded them to be baptized in the name of the Lord." On several occasions Paul "persuaded" people (see Acts 19:8, 26; 26:28; 28:23). An evangelistic invitation is a form of persuasion. Baptism stood for about the same thing in apostolic days as coming forward and making an open declaration of faith does today. Baptism was the public line of demarcation between the old life and the new in New Testament times, and most certainly called for public confession and personal identification with the Christian group. Paul uses strong language and emotion when he recites to the Ephesian elders how "that by the space of three years [he] ceased not to warn every one night and day with tears" (Acts 20:31), and that he had done this "publickly, and from house to house" (Acts 20:20). If he did not use our methods of invitation, he must have had something akin to them. In II Corinthians 5, Paul says, "Knowing therefore the tenor of the Lord, we persuade men," "The love of Christ constraineth us," and, "Now then we are ambassadors for Christ, as though God did beseech you by us: we pray you in Christ's stead, be ye reconciled to God." These are strong terms. In an evangelistic invitation, we do present the constraining love of Christ, and beseech and pray men to be reconciled to God by an immediate surrender and public manifestation of the same.

The last invitation of the Bible, Revelation 22:17, is significant and suggestive, "The Spirit and the bride say, Come. And let him that heareth say, Come. And let him that is athirst come. And whosoever will, let him take the water of life freely." The Spirit says "Come" within the heart and soul of the lost sinner. The bride is the wife of the Lamb and must be the saints, or the Church. The bride says, "Come." The preacher or evangelist voices the invitation of the bride in his evangelistic appeal. All who hear should join in the invitation to come.

Modern evangelistic invitations are of comparatively recent origin, but the spirit and principle of the evangelistic invitation is as old as the Bible itself. The American evangelist, Asahel Nettleton (1783-1844), began using the inquiry room around the year 1817 in connection with what he called "anxious meetings." Many evangelists since have used the inquiry room successfully. The inquiry room offers the best means of separating seekers from others for purposes of instruction and decision. Evangelists D. L. Moody and Major Whittle were known as experts in the use of the inquiry room. The practice arose of asking people to go into the inquiry room either after the benediction or during the closing invitation period.

Evangelist Charles G. Finney first used the "anxious seat" in the Rochester, New York, revival of 1831. He had certain seats reserved near the front for those willing to admit that they were under conviction and anxious about their souls. A first step toward conversion was to sit on the "anxious seat." Finney often addressed some of his sermon to the people on the "anxious seat." His purpose was to bring the unconverted to an immediate decision and to a public commitment.

Both the "anxious seat" and the inquiry room paved the way for various other types of invitations for public declarations, and thus it seems our present-day invitations originated.

2. INVITATIONS ARE LOGICAL

Evangelistic sermons are for the purpose of winning people to Christ. Every effort is made during the evangelistic meeting to create an atmosphere favorable for decision. What better time and place could there be for becoming a Christian than in such a meeting? Why not ask for the decision immediately? Favorable inclinations may soon pass away if people leave the meeting without acting upon these highest impulses. Satan will soon snatch the Word from their hearts and fill their thoughts with other matters when they have left the meeting.

We live in a day of skillful and high-pressure advertising. People are accustomed to all kinds of appeals. Radios, newspapers, magazines and billboards bring a flood of solicitations to see and to buy. Salesmen ask us to sign on the dotted line when their sales appeal ends. Our generation is perhaps more invitation-minded in this respect than any other has ever been. We should utilize this invitation-consciousness at every favorable evangelistic opportunity.

Evangelistic meetings in our day have educated people to expect the invitation at the close of the Gospel message. Some persons may feel that they cannot become Christians unless the opportunity is offered them to take a public stand for Christ. We should not disappoint any such. We are free from the blood of all men, as far as public ministry is concerned, when we give a clear, urgent and warm-hearted evangelistic invitation.

3. INVITATIONS ARE PSYCHOLOGICAL

They are supported by the best principles of modern psychology. Emotions aroused and desires stirred will soon pass away unless acted upon at once. Good impulses are harder to generate the second time than they were the first time if the first impulse did not result in action. The old proverb, "Strike while the iron is hot," applies in giving evangelistic invitations. One of the reasons why our movies and radio dramas usually have a bad effect is because they stir the emotions to a high pitch and do not offer any practical outlet for action. An evangelistic sermon delivered in the power of the Holy Spirit arouses the very highest emotions, aspirations and desires — God Himself moves mightily upon men. Is it not well-nigh criminal if we fail to give opportunity for public decision? Opportunities to meditate privately upon good impulses, and to take plenty of time to act upon them, are almost a thing of the past. Everyone is busy today. Many things press upon us. Calls for our time and attention are multitudinous. Decisions for Christ must be made while people are in a favorable mood and in a spiritual environment or they may never be made.

4. INVITATIONS ARE PRACTICAL

They are historically justified. They accomplish the main end of the Gospel, namely, to win men to Christ at the earliest moment. Every outstanding evangelist in America for the last hundred years has used invitations of some kind. Men owned of God like Finney, Moody, Torrey, Chapman, Sunday, Gipsy Smith and Biederwolf believed in and used the evangelistic invitation. Most successful evangelistic churches support the use of the evangelistic invitation.

People need a definite and vital Christian experience. If they are brought into church membership by infant baptism, or through catechetical classes, or by some private meeting with a membership committee, they are less likely to be certain of their salvation than if they make a personal response to a public evangelistic invitation. Many professing Christians lack assurance of salvation because they cannot recall any time when they made a definite transaction with God. The evangelistic invitation brings the crisis of conscious committal, which is highly desirable. The writer does not insist that a public response is necessary to salvation, but he does believe that such a response, followed by careful personal work, brings most people to a higher degree of assurance of salvation than they would ever have otherwise.

Unsaved people are more inclined to become Christians when they see others taking a public stand for Christ. Sometimes the lost are deeply moved when they see a loved one or friend step out boldly for the Lord. When one person moves forward, it is often possible to persuade others to follow, whereas, if one does not lead the way, no others will make a decision for Christ. The action of one unsaved person in making a public decision for Christ has a salutary influence upon the others. We forfeit this powerful leverage if we give no evangelistic invitations.

Invitations definitely increase the number of conversions and additions to church membership. Dr. William McCarrell, pastor of the Cicero Bible Church, near Chicago, attests this fact. This church is one of the greatest Bible-teaching and evangelistic churches in the United States. It has grown to this place under the evangelistic ministry of Dr. McCarrell. He says that previous to 1922 he either did not give invitations at all, or else merely asked people to raise their hands. In 1922, however, he began asking people to come forward, with the result that there was a greater spirit of revival and the church grew much faster than before. We know that evangelistic invitations tend to sweep in some chaff with the wheat, but we believe this objection can be largely eliminated if we deal carefully with inquirers. All methods of receiving church members let in some unsaved persons. Non-evangelistic churches have a larger percentage of unsaved people in them than evangelistic churches have.

In spite of all we have said in favor of invitations, we know some good, sincere Christians do not believe in them. Such people hold that if we preach the Gospel faithfully, the unsaved will hear, believe and be saved without any inducements to make a public declaration. A prominent fundamentalist Presbyterian minister answered the inquiry of a student in the Northern Baptist Theological Seminary as follows:

> Since I find no Scriptural basis for an invitation to accept Christ and since I believe that it is contrary to New Testament teaching, I do not use the invitation. It is the Holy Spirit working in the hearts through the preaching of the Word that will bring an outward manifestation of either inquiry or confession. In my meetings I invite anyone who is interested to speak to me after the meeting and then I leave the matter with God, confident that He is able to convict and draw without human coercion and that not a soul will leave the meeting whom He would have born again. In other words, it is simply a matter of preaching the Word faithfully and resting in the knowledge that His Word will not return to Him void, nor is He ever negligent.
>
> I believe that almost any speaker can so work upon the emotions of an audience, that through an invitation a great display may be achieved but it would be strange if there was not some display since certainly the vast majority of Christians want to be yielded to the Lord, want victory over sin, want to be filled with the Spirit. In the case of the unsaved, an emotional appeal coupled with the impression that by raising the hand or standing heaven is gained and hell is forever behind them, is, of course, likely to get gratifying results.

Note that this brother does give the invitation to meet him privately after the meeting. Evidently he is not so much against invitations as he is against high-pressure appeals which sweep people into a public commitment that they are not spiritually prepared to make. We sympathize with that view. However, we have noticed that some of these friends who are against public evangelistic invitations go to almost any length using the appeal in personal evangelism. If it is right to plead with a single sinner to repent and receive the Lord Jesus Christ, why is it not right to plead with a whole audience to do the same? The evangelistic invitation has more than demonstrated its value when used by Spirit-filled men. God has honored and blessed its use in bringing untold millions of people into a genuine conversion experience. We freely admit that God is able to save individuals without the use of any human means, and He may do it at times, but it seems that such cases are exceptional. God uses saved people to reach unsaved people. He ordains and blesses various means, instruments and methods in evangelizing a lost world, and the evangelistic invitation is one of the means He has chosen to use.

2

HOW TO GIVE INVITATIONS

THE invitation is the most important and exacting part of the evangelistic service. The crucial test of all that has gone before comes in the invitation. Many prepare the evangelistic message well, but make the mistake of giving no forethought to the invitation. As the salesman studies how to persuade his prospective customer to sign on the dotted line, as the lawyer studies how to secure a verdict for his client, as the fisherman studies how to land his fish after he has a strike, even so must the Gospel preacher study how to secure an adequate response to the evangelistic message. We hope the following general suggestions may prove valuable.

1. GIVE THE INVITATION CLEARLY

Do not confuse people by mixing propositions. It is one thing to come forward to confess Christ as Saviour and Lord, and another thing to come forward for restoration from backsliding or for reconsecration, and still another thing to come forward to apply for membership in the church. Each proposition should be stated specifically and clearly separated from other propositions. Nothing could be much worse than to have people coming forward without knowing just what the step means. Several propositions may be made at one time if each one is carefully explained.

2. GIVE THE INVITATION CONFIDENTLY

Timidity will defeat an invitation. Neither should there be an attitude of carelessness, indifference or uncertainty as the appeal is made. Do not say, "Is there one who will raise the hand for prayer?" Say, "How many are there here who will raise the hand for prayer?" If there is any lack of confidence on the part of the preacher, he should not betray it during the invitation. Confidence is always present when we know someone will respond. Therefore, many evangelists and pastors always try to have a definite understanding with someone in the audience that he is ready and willing to answer as soon as the appeal goes forth. A good way to show confidence is to come down from the pulpit or platform to the level of the people and stand there to meet the people as they come. This indicates that you expect people to meet you in the invitation. Also, as you get nearer the people, it is somewhat easier for them to come.

3. GIVE THE INVITATION EARNESTLY

Speak as a dying man to dying men. Realize that the eternal destinies of men hang upon the outcome of your invitation. Let all frivolity, jokes, antics and stunts be put aside. The solemnity of eternity should characterize an invitation. Plead for Christ with holy concern and melting compassion.

4. GIVE THE INVITATION COURTEOUSLY

Respect the rights of your hearers. Do not embarrass people by making them conspicuous. Do not resort to tricks or deception of any kind. Let the whole audience know that you wish the coöperation of every one during the invitation. Thank the people for staying with you through a prolonged invitation. Thank the Christians for praying during the invitation. Do not overpersuade. Ask personal workers to be tactful.

5. Give the Invitation Honestly

Keep your promises about the number of songs or stanzas you will sing. Let the people go when you promise. If a break should occur, so that it is desirable to go overtime, apologize and dismiss those who wish to go. Be honest in your propositions. If you indicate that you will not ask people to do anything more than raise their hands, then do not violate your word and ask them to do something more. People judge evangelists and ministers very severely in matters of truthfulness. Give no occasion for criticism.

6. Give the Invitation Optimistically

Be in a good humor. Let the light of Christ dominate your personality. People will be as much impressed by your bearing as by your message. Let nothing upset you or put you in a bad humor. Do not scold, cajole, tease, criticize, castigate, chastise or bully an audience. Your invitation will fail, and people will leave you severely alone after one such treatment. Speak with love, patience, kindness, gentleness and the spirit of Christ. Radiate optimism and Christian good cheer.

7. Give the Invitation Naturally

Do not try to be someone else. Be yourself but be your best self. We hope this book will suggest many methods and ideas from others which you can use, but you had better not try to use the gestures, the tone of voice, the phraseology or the mannerisms of any other person. Let the Holy Spirit use you to the maximum. The Holy Spirit respects our individuality and uses each of us differently. David found he could not use Saul's armor and relied on his own weapon, the sling, which was the most effective instrument for him.

8. GIVE THE INVITATION IN ENTIRE DEPENDENCE UPON THE HOLY SPIRIT

You can do nothing apart from the presence and power of the Holy Spirit. Pray for the Spirit's power, lean upon the Spirit, listen for the Spirit's whisperings. Look for the Spirit's movement in the audience; try to discern the Spirit's promptings regarding every step of the invitation. Do not try to do the work of the Holy Spirit. He alone can convict men of sin and of righteousness and of judgment. He can reveal to sin-blinded minds the value of the finished work of Christ on the Cross. Make room for the Holy Spirit to work. Expect His presence, count upon Him, maintain a life and testimony pleasing to Him and He will not disappoint you. Honor the Holy Spirit by honoring and preaching the Lord Jesus Christ and your ministry will be blessed. The Holy Spirit can be grieved by human pride, human boasting, human display and fleshly reliance upon theatrical tricks. The Holy Spirit uses the Word of God when proclaimed by a man of God. Give the Spirit these channels of power!

9. GIVE THE INVITATION PRAYERFULLY

It is very important to maintain an atmosphere of prayer. We must pray much about our message and our invitation. We can pray as we plead for souls. Mr. Frank Sheriff, chairman of the Christian Business Men's Committee of Chicago, says that the Christians in the audience should unite in silent prayer during the invitation. Sometimes Christians will look around to see what is happening, or be looking out the window, or into their purses, or whispering. We must request Christians to refrain from such distractions and give themselves to earnest prayer while the invitation goes on. If Christians will pray for definite unsaved individuals in the audience they can help much.

10. GIVE THE INVITATION POSITIVELY

Suggest what people need to do, not what they should not do. Let all appeals be in the affirmative. You may help them to make the right decision by saying, "Yes, Lord, I will," "Yes, Lord, I am coming, I am coming now," "Say it, do it, do it now," "Friend, you mean to receive Him some time. Receive Him now. He stands outside the door. Open that door. Say to Him, 'Come in, Lord Jesus, come into my heart. Come in today. Come in to stay.'" Such affirmations and suggestions create positive reactions.

11. GIVE THE INVITATION ENCOURAGINGLY

Encourage people to take some forward step, even though it be only a promise by the raised hand to return to the meeting another night. Do not slam the door of commitment in people's faces by making them think they probably never will have another opportunity to be saved. Show them the danger in delay and postponement, but tell them you hope they will have another chance. Indicate that you are expecting them to make the decision at some other time even though they have not made it now.

12. GIVE THE INVITATION THOROUGHLY

Do not stop too soon, particularly when you know people are present who should make a decision at once. Invitations should not be prolonged to the point of wearing out the audience. On the other hand, hold on as long as there is reasonable prospect of some decision. In many cases it would be better to cut the sermon somewhat shorter and give more time to the invitation. A Chicago Baptist pastor with a true evangelistic passion told the author that he was adopting the plan of cutting down his sermon on Sunday nights to twenty minutes in order to give ten or more minutes to the invitation. Instead of preaching the usual thirty or forty minutes, he makes his sermon more pointed and brief and spends more time pleading the cause of Christ in the invitation. Vary your appeals so as to reach the differing needs of the hearers. Take time enough to press each appeal. Teach the Christian people the necessity of being patient, quiet and prayerful during the appeal. Do not permit the clock to worry you during the invitation. Do not be too long with the invitation, but give the Holy Spirit time to perform His ministry of conviction, wooing and illumination.

13. GIVE THE INVITATION RESOURCEFULLY

Change your methods of giving the invitation. Surprise people with something new from time to time. Think over your invitation beforehand and have three or four plans in mind. When the time comes for the invitation, let the Holy Spirit guide you how to begin and how to proceed through to the end.

14. Give the Invitation Vigorously

Be at your physical best for the invitation. Avoid being worn out, weary, fatigued, worried, preoccupied or indisposed. Concentrate all physical, mental, emotional and spiritual energies upon giving a good invitation. Do not resort to shouting, storming or violent gesticulations, unless that is your natural way of doing other things. "Billy" Sunday's acrobatics were sensational, but natural for him. None of us should try to imitate "Billy" Sunday, but we do need to display strength, poise, vitality and a complete command of the situation. Spurgeon said that a ten-minute nap before the evening message made one a lion in the pulpit. The sight of vigorous manhood on fire for God, pleading humbly but powerfully for Christ, is enough to stir the best emotions and aspirations in hardened hearts.

15. Give the Invitation Scripturally

Hold to the truth of the Word of God in every form of appeal. Quote the Scriptures freely, and rely upon the Word to accomplish the divine purpose. Do not lead people to believe that raising the hand, standing, coming to the front, shaking hands, going into an inquiry room or kneeling at an altar will save them. Faith in Jesus Christ alone brings salvation. People may depend on the means used instead of the end to which the means point—that is, Christ Himself. One can be saved sitting quietly in his seat listening, or saved at home in the privacy of his own room. Invitations have value when they encourage people to initiate action which puts saving faith in motion. However people may go through all the forms and yet not be saved if they are confused about the plain way of salvation. Make everything Biblical and crystal-clear.

16. GIVE THE INVITATION COMPASSIONATELY

Do not be afraid to weep over sinners. Believe that men are lost, condemned, under the wrath of God and in imminent peril every minute they live apart from Christ. Love the souls of men as Christ loved them. Never be professional in the invitation. Pray over the lost until you can feel the pangs of hell laying hold upon them. Yearn for the salvation of the lost even as God yearns for them. Plead as constrained by the love of Christ. Very few men today can plead with power. Is it a lost skill? We must pay a price. We cannot plead unless we bleed—bleed under the burden for souls, bleed with compassion, bleed with tender-heartedness and melting love. One of the most marked impressions of Dr. George W. Truett's preaching and pleading was this yearning solicitude for the lost. Yearning compassion cannot be successfully pretended, assumed, imitated or simulated. It must be genuine. Nothing else can take its place. All begging, haranguing, arguing and fleshly driving are as sounding brass and tinkling cymbals. But holy compassion, flowing from a life of faith and prayer, casts a heavenly glow over one's ministry and leads to a fruitful invitation.

The essentials of a good invitation, then, are numerous. Do not think too much is required for you to begin giving the invitation. All of God's standards are high, but you can give invitations. Pray for God's help. Begin now.

This book is designed to furnish you with a large

choice of plans and methods for giving invitations. The next chapter indicates the various motives to which we may appeal in order to move men. However, we must not rely upon mere cleverness or human skill for invitational results, nor, on the other hand, expect God to do for us supernaturally what He has given us power to do or find out for ourselves. In the matter of invitations then, we should prayerfully select varying methods, modify them as may be wise in a particular situation and use them in reliance upon the Holy Spirit.

Evangelistic sermons should appeal to the different elements of human nature—intellect, emotions and will. The invitation, however, is primarily an appeal to the will. We call for action, and use the very best strategy we know, under God, to get a favorable response immediately.

3

HOW TO APPEAL TO VARIOUS MOTIVES

THE evangelistic invitation is an appeal to the will for decisive, wholehearted and immediate action. The influences or motives that move the will are not the same with all people. We have a right to appeal to all the various incentives that may bring action, provided the appeal is on a high moral level and is consistent with the truth and dignity of the Gospel of Jesus Christ. Paul said, "I am made all things to all men, that I might by all means save some" (I Corinthians 9:22). Here are some of the motives, incentives, stimuli to which we may appeal as we seek to bring about the most important of all decisions.

1. THE APPEAL TO SAVE THE SOUL

Man is lost, perishing, condemned, and is in imminent peril every moment he lives without Christ. His eternal soul is at stake. The destiny of his soul is in his own hands as far as accepting or rejecting its salvation is concerned. "For what shall it profit a man, if he shall gain the whole world, and lose his own soul?" asked Jesus (Mark 8:36). On the day of Pentecost Peter urged, "Save yourselves from this untoward generation" (Acts 2:40). This is the appeal to fear, and is frowned upon by some. But fear is a powerful motive for good in human life, and this appeal will move some where

other appeals will not. Hell and eternal condemnation
are Biblical truths. Death is on every hand. If facing
these facts will scare some into seeking the Lord, then
it had better be that way than to miss the kingdom
altogether.

2. THE APPEAL TO FIND RELIEF, RELEASE AND REST

The unsaved person does not know real rest and
peace. His life is out of harmony with the highest
realities. Earthly satisfactions are never deep or long-
lived. When the Holy Spirit begins to convict of sin,
righteousness and judgment, restlessness, dissatisfaction
and pressure increase until the burden becomes well-nigh
unbearable. Then is the time to use the appeal of Jesus,
"Come unto me, all ye that labour and are heavy laden,
and I will give you rest" (Matthew 11:28).

3. THE APPEAL TO LIVE ON LIFE'S HIGHEST LEVELS

Many are living defeated lives, broken and crushed by
sinful habits and vicious lusts. There is often a sincere
desire to be free and to experience mastery over the
lower self. Timidity, fear and misgiving grip such persons. They can no longer trust themselves to be good
and virtuous, and they doubt that there is any help for
them. Show them the delivering, victorious Christ, able
to set men free and keep them by His power. This is
the appeal to aspiration, and will often reach young
people more effectively than any other appeal. "If the
Son therefore shall make you free, ye shall be free indeed," is the encouraging word of Jesus in John 8:36.
"I can do all things through Christ which strengtheneth
me," is the triumphant shout of Paul in Philippians
4:13. The desire to scale the heights of moral achieve-

ment, the urge to completion, the drive to perfection of character can have some measure of realization for the Christian but never for the lost sinner.

4. THE APPEAL TO YIELD EVERYTHING TO GOD'S LOVE

The love of God has been supremely, convincingly, finally, eternally and overwhelmingly demonstrated in the Cross of Christ. Christ died for us while we were yet sinners, even His enemies. Love sent Christ into the world to die for the perishing, the just for the unjust, that He might bring us to God. How can anyone reject such love? Love yearns to enfold its object in eternal embrace. Do not reason how or why, but surrender to that love. This is probably the most widely used and effective of all appeals.

5. THE APPEAL TO HIGHEST DUTY

God "now commandeth all men every where to repent" (Acts 17:30). It is our duty to do what is right by our fellow men, and it is our highest duty to do what is right by God. Man's first sin is against God. We owe it to God, to others and to ourselves to accept the gift of God which is eternal life through Jesus Christ our Lord. Some people would not think of being discourteous, rude or neglectful toward their neighbors, yet they positively dishonor, grieve and offend Almighty God by ignoring His command to repent and spurning His many offers of eternal salvation. The appeal to duty may reach some of these persons.

6. THE APPEAL TO SET THE BEST EXAMPLE

No man lives unto himself or dies unto himself. Everyone has more influence over some lives than any other person has. When one decides to become a Christian he influences others in that direction. His decision may count not only for himself but for several others who wish to go along with him. The decision against Christ may keep others out of the kingdom. Studies show that when both parents are Christians, usually all of the children will be Christians; and when only one parent is a Christian, about half the children become Christians and half do not. Each one is his brother's keeper. How often it occurs in evangelistic meetings that if one person steps out for a public declaration of intention to become a Christian, several others will follow. The best example any of us can set before his family, his friends, his neighbors, his business associates and strangers is to become a Christian and live wholly for Christ.

7. THE APPEAL TO FOLLOW OTHERS

The hesitating person may be willing to become a Christian if others lead the way. Why allow others to find a greater joy, possess a greater hope and experience a greater grace than you? What is good for others is good for you. What God is doing for others He will do for you.

8. THE APPEAL TO NOBLEST SERVICE

By becoming a Christian, one is able to render the highest possible service to his fellows. He is in a position to pray for them effectively, minister to them helpfully in the Name of Christ, lead them into the Christian life and teach them the things of God from personal experience. The service of Christ affords the deepest satisfaction and lasting pleasure. God often uses humble instruments in a striking way. You do not know what God may do through you until you give Him a chance. Other service is for time and its rewards are soon gone, but Christian service is for eternity and its rewards abide forever. Christ invites your service and needs it. You need to know the joy of His salvation and the possibilities of growth and satisfaction in His service.

9. THE APPEAL TO GRATITUDE

It is only common gratitude to accept an offered gift and to express thanks for it. Have you ever thanked Christ for dying for you? Have you ever thanked God for His love in sending His only begotten Son to provide your salvation? What must God the Father think of the ingratitude of those who ignore His great plan of salvation and go selfishly and smugly on their own way? The rejection of a gift is a cutting offense among friends. The gift of eternal salvation is yours for the taking. Gladly receive and thankfully acknowledge this gift.

10. THE APPEAL TO HONEST INVESTIGATION

One has only to give the Christian life an honest trial to prove that it is the best life. If there are doubts, misapprehensions and hesitations, accept the challenge of Jesus in John 7:17, A.S.V., "If any man willeth to do his will, he shall know of the teaching, whether it is of God, or whether I speak from myself." If the Bible is right, and the Christian is right, then the unbeliever is wrong and has everything to lose in this life and the life to come. If the skeptic, atheist and infidel should be right, and they absolutely are not right, then the Christian is still ahead for he has more joy and satisfaction in this life than the others have. Christ validates every claim He makes for this life, but we must put Him to the test. He certainly will validate every claim He has made for the next life.

11. THE APPEAL TO THE NEED FOR FRIENDSHIP

The world is full of lonely people, but one need never be lonely if he knows Jesus Christ as Saviour and Lord, for He is the friend that sticks closer than a brother. Jesus said, "Henceforth I call you not servants [slaves]; for the servant knoweth not what his lord doeth: but I have called you friends; for all things that I have heard of my Father I have made known unto you" (John 15:15). Christ is the true friend for every time of need. More than that, the friends of Christ are the friends of the Christian. Christian friendship and fellowship is the nearest approach to heaven on earth. Christian people are the best people in the world. A few of them as friends are worth more than a host of worldly friends. If you fear losing some of your sinner friends in becoming a Christian, be assured that you will gain more and better friends as you serve Christ.

12. THE APPEAL TO LOGIC AND REASON

This appeal might summarize all the others. There is every good reason for being a Christian and none for remaining in sin. Marshal the reasons and appeal to good sense, sound logic and sane judgment. This appeal will not move many people, but it will be fruitful with some. Even here, the Holy Spirit must back up our reasoning by His mighty power. Charles G. Finney is an example of one who appealed to reason and won thousands to Christ. He arranged his arguments in logical legal fashion and made powerful appeals to the will. Isaiah, speaking for Jehovah, says, "Come now, and let us reason together, saith the Lord: though your sins be as scarlet, they shall be as white as snow; though they be red like crimson, they shall be as wool" (Isaiah 1:18).

This list does not exhaust all the possible motives to which we may appeal, but includes the ones most generally used, and shows that we need to be resourceful in the evangelistic appeal.

4

WHEN TO GIVE INVITATIONS

IN SOME churches, it is the custom to give the invitation at every service. An evangelistic emphasis is maintained throughout the year. This is the most healthy and profitable type of evangelism, but there are other churches where it would be folly to give the invitation at every service, or even every Sunday night. Good sense and spiritual discernment should guide us when to give the invitation, and when not to give it. Certainly the invitation should not be given in a matter-of-fact mechanical manner. If it is given at all, let it be given as indicated in the previous chapter.

The invitation should usually be given when you know there are unsaved people present. Invitations are primarily for lost persons, and when they are in a service they should be challenged to become Christians then and there. Someone may respond even though the sermon has not been evangelistic. We cannot tell what point of truth the Holy Spirit may use to open a human heart to God. If the preacher knows that no unsaved people are in his audience, he may well omit the invitation, and exhort the Christians to apply the truth to their own lives in private dedication.

In evangelistic meetings, it is sometimes better to give the invitation the first night than to wait until a week later. This is especially true if the first night is a Sunday night. You may have more unsaved people in the meeting the first night than you will have any other night for a week or two. Let circumstances guide you.

Give the invitation when you are reasonably certain of even one response. Do not reap all the harvest at one time if it is possible to spread it out over several times. If there is a person present ready to join the church by letter, give the invitation. Do not wait to have several people come at the same time. When one person comes, another whom you do not expect may come. It is better to have a few decisions in several different services than to have many at one service and none at the other services.

Give the invitation when you sense the convicting presence and power of the Holy Spirit upon the audience. This may occur at unexpected times. Be ready to thrust in the sickle when the Spirit breathes upon you and your congregation. On some occasions, contrariwise, you will feel a spirit of coldness, prayerlessness and hardness in the service. Such is not a good time to give the invitation. A few voluntary prayers or testimonies from the people may change the whole atmosphere and make it appropriate to give an invitation.

A preacher can usually tell when he is preaching with freedom and power, and know whether an invitation is suitable after his sermon. On the other hand, we ministers are not infallible judges of the effectiveness of our messages. Occasionally, when we feel our message has been a failure, weak and powerless, God surprises us by giving us decisions. Some of our best sermons, ones which we delight to preach, may not bring any responses. Again, we say, depend on the Holy Spirit and let Him lead. But if we give the invitation fruitlessly on one or more successive occasions, we should not cease to give it. The next time may be the time that tells.

One man can sometimes give the invitation and save the situation for another man, if two preachers are working together. The preacher of the evangelistic message should generally give the invitation, but there may be exceptions to this rule. A congregation is likely to have more confidence in their pastor than in anyone else, and he can frequently give the invitation with results when another man has failed.

The invitation is no problem when a genuine spiritual awakening prevails. When revival seasons come upon a church or community, it is not hard to bring the lost to a decision for Christ. Then it is that sinners turn to the Lord in the church and out of the church. When the Holy Spirit works in the floodtide of revival blessing, any kind of an invitation will bring results; in fact, people will be saved without any invitations.

The goal of all evangelism should be, and perhaps is, to bring about true revival. The sad fact is, however, that most evangelism does not operate in a revival atmosphere. Evangelism today is usually too circumscribed to attain revival levels. Our campaigns are limited to certain set dates; only a small portion of the Christians back the campaign with prayer and personal work; the attendance on week nights is distressingly small; unsaved people rarely come several nights consecutively, and thus they lose the cumulative effect of the meetings; and too much dependence has to be put upon advertising, organization and human leadership. But God blesses our evangelistic campaigns, nevertheless, and we do reach some of the lost. Some churches would never make any progress if it were not for the annual evangelistic campaign. Invitations are a necessary part of evangelism. Unsaved people are perishing every day all around us, and much as we desire great revivals, we must not wait helplessly until revival comes. We must evangelize while we pray for and hope for revival.

5

SIXTY-FIVE WAYS TO GIVE
EVANGELISTIC INVITATIONS

VARIETY and resourcefulness are invaluable assets of
the evangelistic preacher. By falling into fixed and
mechanical ways of conducting public services, he fails
to make the best use of his opportunities, and may frus-
trate the delicate leadings of the Holy Spirit. Therefore,
the Gospel preacher should be informed about the many
ways by which invitations may be given, so that he may
keep his services varied and interesting. Everything
should be done in decency and order, of course, and
in harmony with the truth and dignity of the Gospel.
We should, however, avoid a dead sameness and mo-
notonous repetition. God is a God of infinite diversity
as seen in His works in both the natural and spiritual
worlds.

We make no claim that every evangelistic preacher
should use all of these invitational methods, nor do we
infer that all are of equal merit. We have drawn up
the experiences of successful soul-winners, and have
made suggestions from our own observation and experience, with the hope that we might give help to all
who wish to improve their invitational techniques. Every
reader is at liberty to use anything he wishes from this
book and ignore the rest.

All sincere servants of Christ oppose cheap methods

of sensationalism, trickery, high-pressure, deception and claptrap. Evangelism has been dishonored and discredited too often by such tactics. The Holy Spirit cannot honor methods unworthy of the Gospel of Christ. Too many evangelists and preachers have been more interested in numbers than in quality of conversions. We wish to emphasize that these methods of giving evangelistic invitations are not written with the idea of helping these number-getters herd unconverted people into the churches. But, like Paul, we must be made all things to all men that we might by all means win some (I Corinthians 9:22). If this book can inspire only one preacher to give better invitations and thus turn more people to Christ, we shall count it worth while.

No two people are exactly alike. We differ in personalities, temperaments, abilities, mannerisms, training and theological views. We believe every minister of the Gospel can discover some invitations in this book that he will approve and wish to use. Perhaps there will be others which will not appeal to him at all. This is to be expected. Let each advocate of salvation select and utilize those methods by which he can do his best for Christ.

Situations differ, and congregations differ. Some of these invitations could not be used in certain churches without arousing criticism. Other invitations herein are too weak and mild for some places. Even in a particular church, circumstances will vary considerably. In the heat of an intense evangelistic campaign, vigorous persuasion and pleading will be in order, while at other times such pressure will be inappropriate and injurious.

The main concern is to win as many people to Jesus Christ as possible, and to secure definite public declarations for Him as often as possible. The evangelistic harvest does not ripen all at one time like a field of grain, but some of it is ripening all the time. We must reap whenever and wherever there is any ripened grain. In any evangelistic service, people may be ready to decide for Christ if given the opportunity. We should believe in the possibility of instantaneous conversions at any time. What a pity it is to let anyone leave uncommitted who would have made a decision if the proper invitation had been given! When the Gospel is preached faithfully, and an urgent invitation given, the blood of the lost is no longer upon the preacher.

Man cannot do the work of God, neither will God by Himself do the work He has given man to do. God through the Holy Spirit convicts, converts and regenerates, but God will not reveal directly to any person the type of invitation to use if He has made it possible for that person to find out that same thing in other ways. The Holy Spirit can do more with us if we are equipped and prepared to use methods which the Spirit has blessed in similar circumstances with other servants of God.

Of one thing we can be certain: the Gospel deserves a response. Christ's call to men expects an answer. We should preach for a verdict just as a lawyer pleads with a jury for a decision in favor of his client. That is the best preaching which intends to change lives and change them now. We seek to confront men with Christ and His claims in such persuasiveness that they will yield to Him unreservedly. That is evangelistic preaching; and evangelistic preaching culminates in a cogent appeal for immediate action.

While some people would undoubtedly be saved

without any invitation being given, yet others apparently never would be saved apart from a definite public appeal. This writer doubts that he would have been saved when he was if a forceful invitation had not been given. On that night the pulpit invitation was not enough. The minister did the unusual thing of coming down into the audience to the seat where this sin-burdened lad of thirteen years stood, and took him by the hand and invited him to come to the front and seek the Lord. He yielded to that fatherly entreaty, and that night passed out of the kingdom of darkness into the kingdom of the Son of His love. Unsaved people rarely look for a way to accept God's call, but rather a way to escape it. Men are running away from God rather than to Him. We must shut up the ways of escape and hedge these sinners in to the straight and narrow way which leads to life eternal. Learn to give invitations; learn to give them appropriately, wisely and effectively. Learn by practice the meaning of Paul's word in II Corinthians 5:20, "Now then we are ambassadors for Christ, as though God did beseech you by us: we pray you in Christ's stead, be ye reconciled to God."

Wise fishermen take a wide selection of baits and casting plugs in their kits. They know which baits should attract the fish, but fish are extremely unpredictable. Several changes of bait will often be made before the fish begin to strike. Christ has called us to be fishers of men. Some will use only the rod and reel of personal evangelism. Others must throw out and haul in the Gospel net in public evangelism. Let us learn all we can about how to do it.

For convenience in using these invitations, we have classified them into general groupings. We have arranged them in a progressive order of difficulty from the easiest to the hardest to give, and also from the easiest to the hardest to which to make response. This arrangement may seem somewhat arbitrary, and we admit that it is, but we hope it will be useful to the reader in selecting the invitation he may wish to use on any particular occasion.

A. INVITATIONS TO MAKE THE DECISION LATER

We consider this the mildest form of invitation. On some occasions, this form of invitation may be the best to give. It is hardly virile enough for the average evangelistic service.

1. *Invite those concerned about their souls to come to the pastor's study the following day.* Ask those concerned about their souls' welfare to come to the pastor's study at a certain time tomorrow for conference and prayer; or, set the same time for the next several days. Pray definitely for certain people by name, asking the Lord to send them to the study at the appointed time. Claim them for Christ by faith and prayer. Be at the study at the time appointed, and even ahead of time, for some might come early if the Spirit is dealing with them. Be prepared to show them the Scripture passages dealing with salvation and assurance. Put the Bible in the inquirer's hand and let him read the designated passages aloud slowly; question him about them; apply them to him personally until the light breaks. Then lead him in a prayer of simple, earnest committal to the Lord. Be certain each inquirer has assurance of salvation before he leaves the study. Then urge him to make a verbal confession at some public service at the earliest possible

moment, in accordance with Matthew 10:32-33 and Romans 10:9-10. If several come at the same time, they can be handled as a group, but it is better to deal with them one at a time. In any case, be sure to pray with them and have each one pray for himself.

2. *Instruct those under conviction to settle their problem at home.* Instruct those under conviction to go home and make their commitment in the privacy of their own closets, then come early before the next service begins and tell you what they have done. Tell them how to use such passages as John 1:12, John 5:24 or John 6:37 as the basis for their committal. Explain that they must make a definite acceptance of Christ, and claim salvation solely on the basis of God's Word, and not depend on their emotions. This invitation may appeal particularly to timid and retiring persons, who naturally hesitate to take any public stand. Even then, when one does receive Christ according to this plan, he should follow through with a public confession. The public confession is much easier to make after a person has committed himself to Christ and received the assurance of salvation, than it is to contemplate making before one takes such a step. D. L. Moody tells us that he gave an invitation similar to this the night of the historic Chicago fire of 1871. After a stirring evangelistic sermon, Moody told the people to go home and think the matter over and come back the next Sunday for a public confession. That night Chicago was reduced to ashes, Moody's meeting place was burned, his congregation scattered and he never saw some of the people again. He says he never gave that type of invitation any more, but thereafter always

urged people to make a decision for Christ immediately. When you use this invitation, you should emphasize the necessity of acting while the impulse is fresh in the mind. Delay is dangerous.

B. INVITATIONS TO SIGN CARDS

Card-signing is perhaps more suitable for large union campaigns than it is for single church meetings, although the registration plan is used in many churches.

3. *Ask the members of the audience to leave signed cards in the pews.* Place registration cards in cardholders or in the hymnbook racks on the backs of the pews. After the message, while the people are still seated, ask everyone to sign a card as a matter of recording attendance. Have an invitation hymn played softly and give people ample time to sign. The cards should contain lines for name, address, telephone number, place of church membership, first decision for Christ, renewal of former decision, application for baptism and request for transfer of church membership. This method will not embarrass those registering decisions since everyone will be required to record his attendance. Tell the audience to leave the cards in the pews or card-holders; or a better way may be to have all the cards passed down to the ends of the pews and collected by the ushers before the benediction. Cards marked for any kind of a decision should be followed by personal calls, and each person given all the information necessary to establish him in salvation and assurance. Quite a few city churches register the congregation every Sunday at the time the announcements are made. This is one of the very best ways to compile an active prospect list.

4. *Invite those interested to raise their hands if they desire decision cards.* Ask the people to bow their heads in prayer and keep them bowed while you give the invitation. Tell them the ushers have decision cards which they will give to anyone who raises his hand. Have the ushers move slowly up and down the aisles, as the invitation hymn is played softly, and as you plead quietly for decisions. As hands go up and receive the cards, ask people to sign them and hand them to an usher or to you after the benediction. The next day all those who signed cards should receive personal visits.

5. *Invite those interested to sign cards after the benediction.* Suggest that after the benediction, interested persons present signed cards to the minister as they leave the building. If anyone hands you a card, look at it to see if you need more information before he leaves.

All card-signing should be regarded only as a first step. Every signer should receive a personal interview at an early date. If there is any uncertainty regarding personal salvation, this matter should be adjusted first of all. Obligations of the Christian as to baptism, church membership, stewardship and service should be carefully discussed.

C. INVITATIONS TO REMAIN FOR AN AFTER-SERVICE

After-meetings provide most effective opportunities to deal with inquirers without haste or publicity.

6. *Invite inquirers to remain.* Request the audience to leave the building quietly and without delay, while those anxious about spiritual matters remain behind and gather at the front for prayer and conference. The preacher or evangelist should remain at the front too, so he can en-

courage people to meet him there. Some of the trusted workers should be told beforehand of the plan, and asked to remain also. Their help may be needed.

7. *Invite those desiring spiritual help to gather in the inquiry room.* Tell those who wish spiritual help to gather in some room below or at one side of the auditorium. Someone should be in this room playing the piano softly, and a deacon should stand at the door to guide people into the room. Invite Christians to bring their friends into this room for spiritual counsel. The leader of the meeting should go into this room immediately after the service closes instead of going to the door to shake hands.

8. *Invite Christians to remain for a prayer meeting.* Ask the Christians to stay after the service to pray for the lost. Invite them to bring their unsaved friends into this prayer meeting. Designate the room for the meeting, or hold it in the front of the auditorium. Assure everyone that there will be no embarrassment. Call the meeting to order and ask for the names of persons who should be saved or revived. Ask for the raised hands of any who wish prayer for themselves. Quote or read a few verses of Scripture on prayer, sing a verse of a hymn, then have every one kneel in prayer. Let the prayers go on for some time and then ask the people to be seated. Now ask for the testimonies of any who have been blessed during this prayer meeting, particularly inquiring if any have been saved while the prayers have been offered. Insist that the Christians keep on praying for these unsaved during the night and the next day and on through the days ahead until they are saved.

9. *Invite those desiring spiritual aid to retire to the study during the invitation hymn.* Instead of closing the service as usual, say that the invitation hymn will be sung as the congregation leaves. If the study is convenient to the auditorium, tell people to meet you in the study while the invitation hymn is being sung, or afterward. The choir will remain in place and sing to the end of the invitation hymn, but the people will begin to disperse when the hymn starts. Have a deacon point the way to the study for those who may need direction. Rev. Aubrey P. White, a Baptist pastor, has used this plan successfully.

10. *Invite converts to reveal privately a previous commitment.* This writer has the account of one evangelistic meeting during which the evangelists gave no invitations at any time for people to make a public demonstration. These men proceeded on the theory that people would be converted simply by hearing the Gospel preached. They preached the Gospel clearly and emphatically throughout the meeting, and trusted the Lord to honor His Word. After a few nights, a lady told one of the preachers that she had been saved by listening to the messages. The next night they invited her to come forward for baptism. Several others came, too, all being under conviction. These were asked to remain after the service for instruction. These evangelists encouraged people to come to them after each service and tell how they had been converted by simply believing the Gospel. The meeting resulted in fourteen baptisms and three additions to the church by letter. Perhaps the results might have been more if stronger invitations had been used.

D. INVITATIONS TO RAISE THE HAND

This is one of the easiest and most widely used invitation methods.

11. *Invite those desiring spiritual help to raise their hands for prayer.* In almost every congregation there are men and women who need and desire spiritual help. God's power is always available. While the audience is bowed in prayer, and an invitation solo is being sung or played on the organ, invite all who have burdens which they need Christ's strength to bear, or guilt for which they need His cleansing power, to raise their hands for prayer. Workers should be seated at vantage points in the room so they can see the hands raised. After prayer and the benediction, the workers should meet the persons who raised their hands and offer to help them and introduce them to the minister. Dr. Daniel A. Poling tells of using this method on Sunday nights during his ministry in the Marble Collegiate Church of New York City. The story is in chapter 1 of his book, *An Adventure in Evangelism.* Occasionally he asked people to stand for prayer instead of raising their hands.

12. *After the usual invitation, ask those who did not respond to raise their hands for prayer if they so desire.* After concluding an invitation to come forward, you may feel that others present should make some move for Christ. Address them as follows: "If there are some here who should have come forward on this invitation, but did not, we would like to pray for you before the service concludes. You desire God to keep the door of salvation open for you until you have entered. You do not mean to reject salvation finally, but fully intend

to settle matters with God sometime, even though you did not do so tonight. You would like to be remembered in prayer that you may be spared until you are saved. Raise your hand just now. We will not ask you to do more. It will help you to do that much. Let me see your raised hand just now. Let us pray for you." Keep your promise and do not ask anything further of those who raise their hands, but remember to pray for them. However, a personal approach might be made to these people and an offer of help extended. Once a person has raised his hand for prayer, he finds it somewhat easier to take another forward step on another occasion. This invitation can sometimes change an apparently fruitless service into a fruitful one.

13. *Ask Christians to raise their hands and then extend a similar invitation to the unsaved.* Another variation of this invitation is, while all have their heads bowed in prayer, to ask Christians who wish prayer for unsaved loved ones in the audience to raise their hands. Before you pray for the unsaved loved ones, request those unsaved loved ones to lift their hands to receive Christ now. Press the matter upon the unsaved. Pray for the lost, and if any have raised their hands to accept Christ, invite them to come to the front after the benediction.

14. *Find out who is unsaved.* We should avoid isolating the unsaved, or making them feel conspicuous, but it is sometimes profitable to know exactly how many claim to be Christians and how many do not. Dr. William McCarrell's method is to have every one bow his head and then ask those who are Christians and glad of it to raise their hands and quote John 3:16

with him, keeping the hand raised while they quote the verse. This gives workers plenty of opportunity to see whose hands are not raised. Then he may ask for the hands of Christians who are sorry they became Christians. He says he has given this negative invitation all over the United States, and never yet have any indicated that they were sorry they became Christians. He enforces the point that this is a glorious testimony to the value of Christianity. Everyone who has tried it is glad, and no one is sorry. Then he asks the unsaved if they would not like to be in this company of glad Christians and if so to raise the hand and thereby make a decision to become a Christian.

E. INVITATIONS TO STAND

This invitation is a step beyond the invitation to raise the hand. There are several ways in which it may be used.

15. *Invite the unsaved to stand as an indication that they have accepted Christ.* After the sermon and appeal, request all who are ready now to accept Christ as personal Saviour and Lord to stand and remain standing while you pray for them. Personal workers will note those who stand, and confer with them afterward. Evangelist Gipsy Smith has frequently used this invitation. The writer one time saw Dr. W. B. Hinson, then of Portland, Oregon, use this invitation in the old Moody Church with a number of responses. Christians should always be asked to bow their heads, close their eyes and engage in prayer while such an invitation is being extended.

16. *Invite praying Christians to stand; then extend a similar invitation to the unsaved.* Ask all who are

praying for the salvation of loved ones or friends to stand so that you may pray with them. Before you pray, ask any unsaved in the house who think they may be among those for whom prayer is being made, to stand as an indication that they are grateful that people are praying for them. If anyone thinks he is not an object of prayer, but would like the Christians to pray for him, invite him to stand, too. Pray for all those standing, both Christians and unsaved. Tell the unsaved that everyone would be happy to see them come to the front and settle the matter now. Invite them to the front after the benediction, or while everyone stands and all join in singing the invitation hymn.

17. *Refer to the trial of Jesus Christ.* A unique invitation that could be used once during an evangelistic campaign comes at the close of a sermon on "What Think Ye of Christ?" or "The Trial of Jesus Christ." The sermon weighs the evidence for and against the claims of Christ as found in the New Testament. First, bring in the witnesses against Christ, the atheists, the infidels, the skeptics, the modernists, and quote a few of their statements against Jesus Christ. Do not spend more than ten minutes on this part of the sermon. Then call out the witnesses, one by one, to testify for Christ, the prophets, the apostles, the angels, the Father's voice from heaven, the martyrs, the great Christian leaders and scientists down to the present day.

Tell the audience that it is the jury and will be asked for a decision. J. Gilchrist Lawson's book, *Greatest Thoughts About Jesus Christ,* contains an abundance of material for a sermon of this nature. Now ask all those who believe Jesus Christ was an impostor and a deceiver, and not what He claimed to be, to stand. Perhaps none will stand. If one should stand, thank him for his courage to stand for what he believes, and tell him you have some books you would like to have him read. Then, ask all who believe Jesus Christ is what He claimed to be—the Son of God, the Saviour of the world, very God of very God, with all authority in heaven and on earth—to stand. Usually everyone in the house will stand.

Now is the time to handle this invitation carefully. Say that you deeply appreciate this unanimous vote of confidence in Christ and His claims. Show that everyone who believes in the deity and Lordship of Christ should also accept Him as Saviour and Lord now. God holds people responsible for what they know. He has the power to save them now, but if they do not receive Him, He has authority to judge them hereafter. Some are now taking more of a public stand for Christ than they probably have ever taken before. Why not go all the way and receive Him as Saviour and Lord? Explain that those who have never trusted Christ before as Saviour and Lord, but wish to do so now, will please remain standing for prayer, while those who have previously trusted Him and confessed Him publicly, will be seated. It is easier to remain standing once they are in that position than it is to rise after being seated. Plead at this point. Show how easy it will be to remain standing for Him who died for us all—if they confess Him before men, He will confess them before the Father in heaven. Entreat them not to sit down if they have never confessed Him publicly before. Pray for those who remain standing and follow them up by personal conferences.

Another possibility, when all are standing, is to invite those who have never personally received and acknowledged Christ before men to come to the front during the invitation hymn. The writer knows a pastor-evangelist who uses this invitation in most of the evangelistic campaigns he holds, and generally has splendid results.

18. *Invite people of various ages to stand.* In the appeal, emphasize the value of making a decision for Christ as early in life as possible. Explain how it becomes harder and harder to become a Christian after one leaves childhood. Demonstrate what you mean by asking those who became Christians after fifty years of age to stand and remain standing a few moments. Count them. Very few will stand. Ask them to be seated. Then ask in turn those who became Christians between forty and fifty, thirty and forty, twenty and thirty, fifteen and twenty, ten and fifteen, and under ten to rise. Each group sits before the next one rises. Most people will rise with younger age groups. This plan used in large congregations shows quite effectively the wisdom of making the Christian decision in life's tender years.

Now take the same groups in reverse order, asking those who became Christians under ten years of age to stand again. Invite others in that age bracket who will now become Christians to stand. Announce to those who stand that you wish to meet them after the service. Go through all the age groups in the same way. Remind all who have stood that you wish to meet them, along with the Christian workers, either at the front or in some side room, after the service. Dr. W. E. Biederwolf's book, *Evangelism,* suggests this method.

19. *Employ Finney's dramatic invitation.* Evangelist Charles G. Finney in his autobiography tells about an unusual invitation he used during his early ministry at a place called Evans' Mills, in Jefferson County, New York. After he had preached several nights without any apparent results, he gave a pointed message one night on Genesis 24:49, and closed by asking all who would give their pledge to make peace with God immediately to stand; but, on the other hand, all who were resolved not to become Christians, and wished Finney to so understand and Christ to so understand, to remain seated. No one stood. He told them that he understood them to mean that they rejected Christ and His Gospel, and would not have Him to reign over them. Why should he remain among them if that was the way they felt? When he pressed them, they began to look angry, and stood up, en masse, and started for the door. Finney now told them that he was sorry for them and would preach to them once more on the next night, the Lord willing.

A deacon came to Finney and told him he had done the right thing. Finney and the deacon agreed to spend the next day in prayer, separately in the morning and together in the afternoon. People were angry throughout the neighborhood, but filled the church the next night. Finney preached a sermon that night under the power of the Holy Spirit. He took it for granted all through the sermon that the people were committed against the Lord and he did not ask them to reverse their decision that night. Deep conviction fell upon individuals all over the community during that night and the next day. A great revival ensued.

Most of us cannot afford to make any proposition that

offends people. Paul says, "Give none offence, neither to the Jews, nor to the Gentiles, nor to the church of God" (I Corinthians 10:32). Finney was definitely depending on the Holy Spirit for guidance, and God blessed his strange procedure. The same Holy Spirit may direct any of us to do the unusual, but let us be certain the Holy Spirit is leading us, and not the inordinate desire for notoriety and publicity.

F. INVITATIONS TO PRAY AT ONE'S SEAT

20. *Invite those desiring prayer to stand while others pray for them.* Dr. Charles E. Goodell in *Pastoral and Personal Evangelism* suggests asking the audience to bow or kneel in prayer. Then ask those who wish prayer to stand. Have several Christians pray specifically for those who stood. Then approach them personally after the service.

21. *Utilize Elder Knapp's prayer plan.* Elder Jacob Knapp, famous Baptist evangelist of the past century, writes that his plan was to have everyone, both saints and sinners, go to their knees in prayer, and to cry to God until He sent down salvation. The converted, in this case, would rise and give thanks to God for saving them. Elder Knapp used this method in what he called "the anxious room," and says he has known fifty persons to be converted in one season of prayer. The same procedure could be followed in any meeting by setting aside a ten-minute period for prayer for the lost. Tell the Christians to pray to God to save the lost right now, while the lost pray silently or audibly, as they may wish, for God to save them now. Instead of having a forty-five minute preliminary service of songs and announce-

ments, we might have more spiritual power in a meeting if we used a part of that time for a prayer service of this character.

22. *Employ Dr. Chafer's invitation.* Dr. Lewis Sperry Chafer, in his book *True Evangelism,* advises extreme caution and care in giving invitations lest we become more spectacular than spiritual, and lest our hearers become confused as to what the actual requirements for salvation are. He recommends that, after the way of salvation has been explained carefully and fully, the whole audience engage in a season of silent prayer. During this time of prayer, the leader urges the unsaved to receive the Lord Jesus Christ by a conscious act of the will as they lift their hearts in silent prayer to God. Those who do this should then make an immediate public confession of Christ by coming to the front, or rising and making a public statement.

The value of this method, he points out, is that people confess that they have already believed in Christ and accepted Him, whereas, otherwise, they might think they were making the confession in order to be saved. After this there should be a personal conference with all who have made a confession to see that they have a clear understanding of the step taken, and that they receive further instruction and strengthening in the faith. We commend this invitational method.

A similar method was used in Chicago one time by Rev. Harry Lindbloom, now deceased. Mr. Frank Sheriff reported this incident. Mr. Lindbloom asked all the people to bow their heads in prayer while a duet was being sung. He asked them to make whatever decisions God indicated, receive Christ, rededicate themselves to

Christ, forgive others, or any other step to please God. Then he asked for the upraised hands of those who had made some decision. Many raised their hands. He next invited those who raised their hands to make a full confession by coming to the front for a closing prayer while an invitation hymn is sung. Many came.

G. INVITATIONS TO MAKE A VERBAL CONFESSION AT ONE'S SEAT

23. *Provide the opportunity for confession on the basis of Romans 10:9-10.* Preach a sermon on Romans 10:9-10, outlining what must be believed for salvation and why confession with the mouth must be made. Ask everyone in the house, who can honestly do so, to stand and confess Christ in these words: "I am trusting Jesus Christ as my Saviour and Lord." Ask each person to say these exact words, no more, no less, but to speak them without mental reservation. Say that you wish all in the house to make this statement personally and singly, whether they have been trusting Christ seventy years or have just begun to trust Him within the last minute. Encourage the unsaved to rise and make this confession along with others as an indication of their initial commitment to Christ. Scores of Christians can make this confession in a few minutes. See that the confessions are made individually and by rising, not in groups or while seated.

This procedure has a profound effect upon unsaved people. They see the line drawn sharply between themselves and the Christians, and begin to realize their position as lost and away from God more than ever. A desire springs up within them to rise and make this confession too, and then they ask themselves whether they can honestly do so. This train of thought may lead to a committal then and there in order to be qualified to make the confession.

The writer remembers using this invitation one night in an evangelistic meeting in an Illinois town. A cultured and refined lady had come to the meeting from a near-by village. No one knew who she was. She kept her seat during the confession service, and hurried out of the meeting at the close. During that night and the next day she was ashamed and miserable because she could not rise with others and confess Christ as Saviour and Lord. She became deeply convicted of her sin. She was back at the meeting the next night, and could hardly wait until the invitation was extended in order to come forward and take a public stand for Christ. She gave her testimony to the effect the meeting of the previous night had made upon her. The author first saw this plan of invitation used by Dr. William R. Newell in tent meetings in Chicago.

Here is a slightly different way of using this same invitation. After the message on confession, say that you are going to ask everyone to recite a confession together. Tell them that the confession will be this: "I believe that God raised Jesus Christ from the dead, and I am trusting Him as my Saviour and Lord." Explain that, while you wish everyone to make this confession, yet you want only those to do it who can do so honestly and sincerely. Show that Christians can all make this confession, and any unsaved person may enter into the kingdom of God by making this confession unreservedly.

Here is an opportunity to be saved by joining with Christians in making this verbal confession, which Romans 10:9-10 certifies is sufficient for salvation. Ask the unsaved to consider the meaning of these words seriously as you repeat them again. Urge them to join with others now in making this good confession before many witnesses. Say, "Now we are going to begin: everyone together, I believe that God raised Jesus Christ from the dead, and I am trusting Him as my Saviour and Lord." Repeat the words slowly so all can follow. Now, have all bow their heads in prayer, and thank God for all who made this confession. Before you conclude the prayer, while heads are still bowed, ask for the raised hands of any who made the confession for the first time, and pray especially for them.

24. *Challenge people to confess what they believe.* Preach a sermon on the character, work and influence of Jesus Christ. After the sermon appeal to the people to tell what they believe about Jesus, using not more than ten or fifteen words each. After some have spoken, invite others to express their faith, even though they may not agree with the orthodox creeds. Some may believe only that Jesus was a good man, the best teacher, or the world's most perfect example. Ask them to confess that much. Assure them that they will not be criticized or condemned if their statement falls short of accepted orthodoxy. Your purpose is to encourage people to make the first confession of their lives. There is a spiritual and psychological principle that when we confess our faith, that faith becomes stronger and larger. Truth believed and not acted upon is relatively impotent; but truth received and put into action becomes powerful and leads to more truth.

Dr. Henry C. Mabie elaborates this principle in chapter 6 of his book, *Method in Soul-Winning*. He uses an illustration of a man who was skeptical, but did believe that Jesus was the greatest teacher the world ever saw. One of the pastors invited this gentleman to his next prayer meeting to confess his faith in Jesus. The man objected at first, but the pastor told him that he believed more than most people supposed, and urged him to come to church and make the confession. He came, and at a proper time in the midweek service arose, and told why he was there. He confessed that he accepted Jesus Christ as a great teacher, and more than that, as his Master and Saviour. He was practically converted on his feet, and went out of the meeting a different man. The full light had burst upon him as he acted upon the partial light he had.

Also, during such a service, you can invite any unsaved to stand and say, "I here and now receive Jesus Christ as my Saviour and Lord." It is important to put in the word "Lord," for we should receive Jesus not only as Saviour, but as Lord. Much evangelism is weak because it does not emphasize the Lordship of Jesus Christ. If people received Christ not only as Saviour from sin and its guilt, but also as Lord of their whole lives, there would be less backsliding and compromising.

H. INVITATIONS TO COME FORWARD

Most invitations include the request to come to the front. We have a right to expect that much of people who mean business, and with whom the Spirit of God is dealing. We may properly doubt the sincerity of one who is unwilling to come forward. Going forward does not save, but it goes a long way toward overcoming fear, timidity and doubt. There are many ways of giving this invitation. The preacher should come down from the pulpit, or pulpit platform, and stand on a level with the front pews unless this position hides him from part of his audience. This action brings him closer to the people, makes it easier for him to meet them as they come and indicates that he expects people to come.

25. *Invite inquirers to come forward.* After the sermon, announce a good invitation hymn such as "Just As I Am, Without One Plea," "Jesus Is Calling," or "Lord, I'm Coming Home," and invite penitents to come to the front. Usually the invitation should include three classes—those who wish to become Christians, those who wish to renew former vows of allegiance and those who wish to unite with the church. The congregation should always stand during such an invitation hymn. When people come to the front, a cordial welcome should be given them. Inquirers may be asked to sit on the front pew, or kneel at the altar, or pass into an inquiry room, according to the custom of the church.

Sometimes a little child will be the first one to come forward. Receive such a little one in the Name of Christ. Instead of having the child sit down, or pass into another room, have him stand beside you and face the audience. Call attention to the ready response of the child, and ask him a few simple questions, such as, "Do you believe that Jesus died for you? Are you ready to receive Jesus as your Saviour and Lord? Do you believe that He will receive you now? Are you willing to trust Jesus and serve Him as long as you live? Are there other people here whom you would like to have receive Jesus?" Do not ask a child hard questions. The author saw Dr. Reuben A. Torrey deal in this manner with a little boy one night. He lifted the little boy up beside him on the platform, and instructed him how to be saved so that the whole audience could hear. He had the child receive Christ, and skillfully led him on into assurance of salvation, so that he could give a testimony right there. The whole procedure took only three or four minutes, yet it had a remarkable effect on the audience. If the invitation is renewed, others are likely to come.

26. *Invite deacons to lead the way.* If no one comes forward and yet you know there are some present who should come, try asking the deacons to come to the front and stand beside you during the next stanza of the invitation hymn. If a church has deaconesses, invite them to come, too. Why should not the spiritual officers of a church stand with their pastor and support him during the invitation? As they come, or after they come, you can invite others to come with them. A movement forward may be all that is necessary to encourage some to yield to the Spirit and come to the front. Years ago, the author saw Dr. Oliver W. Van Osdel, pastor of the Wealthy Street Baptist Church, Grand Rapids, Michigan, use this method. As soon as he gave the invitation, and the audience stood to sing, the deacons moved out of their places in the audience and lined up on either side of the pastor with their faces to the congregation. This movement gave strength to the invitation, and made it easier for others to come. It was an inspiring sight to see all the deacons there beside their pastor, lending their endorsement to the invitation.

27. *Invite Sunday school teachers to lead.* A similar plan is to ask all the Sunday school teachers present,

who believe in this invitation, to come to the front and face the audience. When they have come, commend them for the important work they are doing, and point out that most additions to our churches come from the Sunday school and are due to the work of faithful teachers. Then ask how many Sunday school pupils wish to receive Christ by coming forward and standing beside their teachers. Teachers are much encouraged and blessed when one of their pupils comes to stand beside them. If there should be no response on the first appeal, ask the teachers if any of them wish to add a word to the invitation. Some of them may speak very tenderly and persuasively. If so, extend the invitation through a few more stanzas of the hymn. When pupils do come forward, ask their teachers to remain during the inquiry meeting while the pupils come into the kingdom.

28. *Invite recent converts to lead.* Ask those who are new in the Christian life, but glad and happy and ready to recommend Jesus to others, to come to the front as an encouragement to sinners to break with sin and become Christians. Invite others to come with them. Ask some of the new converts to give a word of testimony, and renew the invitation.

29. *Invite aged Christians to lead.* When an invitation seems to be failing, try inviting those who have been Christians fifty years or more to come to the front. Say that we wish to know who they are. Invite others to come with them. After they have reached the front, compliment them on their long service for Christ, and ask each one exactly how long he has been a Christian. Now ask these aged saints if any of them

have found the Christian life too hard, too disappointing, or too empty. Inquire whether or not any of them would now wish to renounce Jesus and abandon his Christian hope. This will probably bring strong protests. No, none of them wish to abandon Jesus now. They find Him more precious as the years go by. Let each of them say a few trembling words for Jesus if they wish.

Point out to the audience that these people have had an abundance of time to prove the Lord Jesus Christ. If anybody should know whether or not it pays to be a Christian, these people should. They all join in the invitation and urge others to begin serving Christ now. What better evidence could be produced? Who ever heard of a true Christian giving up his Christian hope on his deathbed? Many skeptics, blasphemers and infidels see the error of their ways when death comes nigh, but Christians always hold fast their hope in life's last hours. There is a reason. Renew the appeal under the added impetus of this demonstration.

30. *Invite comforted ones to come forward.* Following a message on "The Christian Hope," or "The Death of Believers"—if there is no response to the appeal—ask those who have found Christ the best friend when death has visited the home, to come to the front as witnesses to His comforting grace. Invite others to come with them and after them.

31. *Invite newly-won converts to lead.* When you have won someone to Christ by personal evangelism, pledge this person to come forward for a public confession at the next evangelistic service. Tell him that his coming may encourage others to follow him. When

you see this new Christian in the audience ready to come when you make the appeal, you are able to give the invitation with greater confidence and effectiveness. Instruct the personal workers to let you know when they have brought someone with them ready to make a confession. When one has come, plead for another to do the same thing. If some plan to join the church by letter, or by Christian experience, arrange with them to do so in one of the evangelistic services, where their action may open the door for others to move forward for Christ.

32. *Invite all the Christians to come forward to pray.* If the congregation is not too large, invite all the Christians who will to come forward during the last hymn for a season of prayer after the benediction. As Christians are gathering around the front, invite the unsaved to come with them, give you their hand and kneel for prayer and instruction. Care should be taken to guard against leaving a few unsaved persons standing alone. Sensitive persons feel conspicuous and resentful in such a case. However, if the Holy Spirit is really at work in a meeting, this invitation may prove quite successful. The unsaved may have an overwhelming sense of their lost condition as the Christians move out and leave them standing alone. The author has witnessed this invitation produce results on many occasions. It may be used more safely toward the end of a revival meeting than at the beginning. Many things can be done after a meeting reaches a high point of power that would not be well received otherwise.

33. *Invite intercessors to come forward.* Ask those praying definitely for the salvation of loved ones or

friends, to come to the front so that you may help them pray for these people. When they have come, ask them to say for whom they are praying, as a father, a brother, a sister, a son, a friend, or a neighbor. Announce an invitation hymn, and invite any who know they are objects of prayer, to come to the front also for prayer and instruction. Whether any come or not, have the prayer meeting, and show people how to pray for the lost. Dr. W. E. Biederwolf used this method.

34. *Invite those under conviction to come forward and into the inquiry room.* Invite people to come forward during the invitation hymn, receive the pastor's hand and pass into the inquiry room for consultation with personal workers. The inquiry room should be near the front of the auditorium, and one or more persons should be ready to escort inquirers into this room. This is very similar to the plan used at the Moody Church in Chicago. Dr. H. A. Ironside, the pastor of the Moody Church, answered an inquiry about invitations as follows:

> I make it a point always to preach definite Gospel sermons on Sunday evening or other times when the unsaved are likely to be in the audience, and I press the importance of coming to Christ as repentant sinners and trusting Him as the only Saviour.
>
> I am not shut up to any particular methods. I generally ask that we have a moment or two of silent prayer at the close of the message and then request any anxious souls to raise their hands that we may remember them in prayer and thus note who are interested. Following a word of prayer for these, while we sing a closing hymn, I invite those who are really in earnest to come to the inquiry room, where they are dealt with personally. We have found these methods most effective.

35. *Invite the burdened to come forward.* Entreat all who need prayer for themselves or their loved ones to come to the front and kneel for prayer. Emphasize the necessity of asking in order to receive. Say that you are willing to pray with any burdened or troubled soul. Do not be afraid of having too many Christians come. The very movement of a number of Christians to the front may bring some unsaved along. After the invitation has been pressed, dismiss the audience and have an after-meeting with those at the front. Show them how to pray; seek to stir up faith in their hearts. Some people do not get things off their hearts praying alone, but they do receive relief when they pray with others. Many coming with burdens are confused regarding salvation, and can be brought to a new level of faith and assurance by proper instruction at the altar of prayer. Rev. Torrey M. Johnson of the Midwest Bible Church, Chicago, likes this appeal. He prefers to keep inquirers at the front of the auditorium for prayer rather than go into an inquiry room, since he believes that something in the way of helpful atmosphere and spiritual seriousness may be lost by moving into another room. A goodly number of unsaved are among those coming to the front for prayer in this church.

36. *Invite the burdened to come to the mourners' bench.* This appeal is very similar to the preceding one, except in this more emphasis is placed on "praying through." This invitation exhorts people to come to the mourners' bench or altar, for salvation, restoration, or filling with the Holy Spirit. We do not condemn the mourners' bench, unless faulty instruction is given in connection with it, or unless people come to believe

it is the only place where they can be saved. The penitent sinner, or burdened soul, often feels more like dropping to his knees and crying out to God in prayer than standing there before a gazing congregation answering questions. We should point out, however, that prayer in itself does not save, but rather faith and faith alone. Prayer is the best medium for stimulating and exercising faith, but we should instruct inquirers to depend solely on Christ and not on their own praying. Seekers should never be left to struggle alone, but we should give them careful Biblical instruction, showing them how to appropriate and claim salvation and the filling with the Holy Spirit.

In some meetings people return to the altar night after night for a week or two seeking salvation. This author believes that such prolonged seeking is unnecessary and unscriptural. God is ready to save any soul instantly if that one will only accept the free gift of His salvation. We do not have to persuade God by our agonizing and praying to take a favorable attitude toward us. God has been reconciled to sinners by the perfect finished work of the Lord Jesus Christ on the Cross. We beseech men to be reconciled to God, which means to repent and believe. Repentance means to change the mind, to reverse one's attitude toward Christ and the Christian life, to condemn the old way of life in sin and unbelief and to accept the new way of life in Christ Jesus. See Jesus' perfect illustration of repentance in Matthew 21:28-32.

Emotional upheaval may accompany repentance, but repentance is primarily an act of the will. Faith in Christ is trust, reliance, dependence, or committal unto Him. Repentance and faith always go together, even though they are often mentioned separately in the Scriptures. Gospel repentance terminates in saving faith, and saving faith presupposes evangelical repentance. If the saving work of Christ, in providing a completed and perfect atonement, is presented lucidly to sinners, they will find it easy to exercise saving faith in Him. Therefore, we should not make the mistake of urging seeking sinners to "pray through" for something which they may receive instantly if properly instructed.

Seekers commonly try to come into some great emotional experience which they identify with salvation. We do not depreciate the emotional type of conversion experience. The emotional element is dominant in the lives of many persons, and it is not surprising that an emotional crisis accompanies conversion. The danger is that when the emotional crisis has passed, such persons may doubt their salvation, unless faithfully taught. Our object at the mourners' bench, then, should be to present each inquirer the Scriptural facts of perfect, free and immediate salvation. Help the sinner to pray honestly, audibly, and in his own words, renouncing sin and the old life and receiving Christ, salvation, forgiveness and eternal life. By using John 1:12, John 6:37, John 5:24, or similar passages, show the penitent that God has now heard, answered, accepted and saved him, according to His glorious promises. When the inquirer has grounded his salvation securely in the Word of God, and has come into full assurance, he should then make a verbal confession to whatever group may be present.

Persons coming to the mourners' bench for blessings other than salvation, should also receive instruction and help. Praying in faith so as to receive answers means to believe the promises of God, act upon them and claim their fulfillment, regardless of the absence or presence of outward evidences. All evangelical churches could profitably use the altar of prayer, or mourners' bench, if sane and Scriptural conduct were followed.

37. *Employ the solo invitation.* Have a Spirit-filled person sing a solo while the people bow their heads in prayer. Invite those who hear the call of God to rise and come to the front during the solo. Mr. Al J. Conn of the "Old Sunday School" radio program gives a very forceful invitation of this type while a young woman sings, "Precious Lord, Take My Hand."

38. *Utilize a military appeal.* During war times, preach on such topics as "Enlisting for Christ," or "Soldiers of the Cross," and appeal to service men and their relatives. First, invite the Christian service men and women who are not ashamed of Christ to come to the front as a testimony to others. Then invite other service people who wish to enroll in the most victorious of all armies to come to the front.

Another appeal is to invite all fathers and mothers, husbands and wives, brothers and sisters of men and women in military service, who are praying for them and would like to have public prayer offered for them, to come to the front. Many will come, perhaps too many. Now appeal to all those service people who know someone at home is praying for their salvation. Invite them to accept Christ by coming forward. When the invitation has been fully extended to service people, then extend it to include civilians.

39. *Appeal to tithers and soul-winners.* One of our country's prominent and successful evangelists frequently

urges Christians to come forward as an indication that they are ready to begin tithing and soul-winning. He points out that Christians are sinning if they do not tithe or try to win souls. They should ask God's forgiveness and seek restoration from these sins. As this appeal begins to take effect, Christians are revived, the revival spirit rises in the church, and the unsaved begin to come to the Lord.

40. *Extend an invitation to young people.* Ask all those who are now in full-time Christian service, or in preparation for it, to come to the front. Then invite those who have been seriously considering full-time Christian service and feel God's call to it, but who have never publicly dedicated themselves to such service and are now ready to do so, to come to the front and stand with these others. Next, appeal to those young people who have never definitely considered full-time Christian service, but are willing to enter it if God should call them and make it plain to them, to come to the front. By this time quite a number of people will be standing at the front. Congratulate them and commend them. Now, appeal to unsaved young people to receive the Lord Jesus Christ by coming to the front and standing with these others. After each of the appeals, sing a stanza of "A Volunteer for Jesus." Dr. Carl F. H. Henry uses this invitation with excellent results. He purposely omits from this invitation those older people whose Christian lives may have been inconsistent and whose presence at the front might be more of a stumblingblock than a help.

41. *Employ an athletic invitation.* Preach a sermon from an athletic text such as I Corinthians 9:24-27,

II Timothy 2:1-5, or Hebrews 12:1-2. Draw comparisons between the athlete's dedication to and training for his goal and the Christian's relation to Christ. Use some good athletic illustrations. Appeal for a team of nine or eleven men for Christ, men who have experienced Christianity and can recommend it to others. Ask them to come to the front and stand as witnesses. If more than eleven come, welcome them all. Then point out that a team usually has cheer leaders. Cheer leaders are often girls. Are there young women present who know Christ and can witness for Him? Let them come to the front, too; let a dozen come, or more. As these young people bear witness to Christ, and rededicate themselves to Him, invite the unsaved to come to receive Him. Dr. J. C. Massee sometimes uses this invitation.

42. *Appeal for a dedication to Christ and purity.* Another invitation given by Dr. J. C. Massee follows a sermon on "Christ in Our Love Affairs," or, "Are Petting Parties Wrong?" He emphasizes the high standards of purity set by the life of Jesus, and the high standards set for Christians in the New Testament. He invites all saints and sinners alike, now ready to dedicate themselves to Christ and purity for all time, to come to the front. Christians will rededicate themselves to Christ and social purity, while the unsaved receive Christ as Saviour and Lord and dedicate themselves to Christian purity. Most of those who come are Christians, but many unsaved are among them. Dr. Massee has had between eight and nine thousand people respond to this invitation during the years he has been giving it.

43. *Employ the lighted cross invitation.* This appeal could come appropriately after a sermon on "The Meaning of the Cross," or "How the Cross Saves Us." Turn out all lights in the building, except a large lighted cross in front, or a light shining on a cross. Have the people bow their heads in prayer, and as the organist or pianist plays "The Old Rugged Cross," or "Near the Cross," extend the invitation to come forward.

A chalk-talk artist will be able to draw a large cross while the message is being delivered. The lights can all be turned off, except the one illuminating the cross that has just been drawn. Some may find it easier to come forward in the semidarkness of the room than in the glare of a brilliantly lighted room.

44. *Invite those who have assurance of salvation to come forward.* After a sermon on assurance of salvation, invite all who are sure of salvation and grateful for it, to come to the front and take your hand. As they come, invite any who lack assurance of salvation, but wish it, to come to the front and remain. Then invite the unsaved to come.

45. *Extend an invitation from the baptistry.* An invitation is usually appropriate following a baptismal service. The ordinance of baptism is a Gospel sermon in itself. The fundamental truths of the Gospel are symbolized and proclaimed as a candidate goes down into the watery grave of baptism, showing death to the old life, and is raised up again, showing resurrection unto newness of life in Christ Jesus. Many people will attend a baptismal service who do not usually attend church services. They are relatives or friends of some person being baptized, or come out of curiosity.

While standing in the baptistry, after baptizing the last candidate, look up toward heaven and say, "Lord, we have done as Thou hast commanded," and looking toward the audience say, "And yet there is room." Invite those who wish Scriptural baptism to come to the front. With them, invite the unsaved who wish to receive Christ and then follow Him in baptism. Sing as the invitation hymn, "Where He Leads Me," and have one of the deacons stand at the front to receive those who come.

46. *Extend a communion service invitation.* New members are often welcomed into the church at the communion service by receiving the right hand of fellowship. When you invite these new members to come forward, invite all others who wish to join the church to come forward, too; and include any who wish to confess Christ as Saviour.

In some churches, instead of the pastor alone, or the pastor and deacons, welcoming the new members, the whole congregation marches around and shakes hands with them. In this case, you can invite those who are not members of the church, but who believe the new members are doing the right thing and should be congratulated, to come around with the church members. As they come, suggest that the unsaved and unchurched, who are ready to decide for Christ, step aside and remain at the front instead of returning immediately to their seats. Any congregation may well join in welcoming new members now and then. Any movement toward the front is good, and may result in conversions.

47. *Extend a funeral service invitation.* The only Gospel preaching some people ever hear is at funeral

services. They will not come under the sound of the Gospel at other times. Rarely should a funeral message ever be entirely evangelistic, but the evangelistic note is appropriate in practically every funeral sermon. Accepted forms of evangelistic invitations would be out of place at a funeral service, but if the preacher feels especially impressed to appeal to the lost there is a way he can do it. He may have every one bow in prayer and ask the lost to raise their hands, or he may stand by the casket as people pass by and ask those who will receive Christ to take him by the hand.

48. *Extend the "last night" invitation.* On the last scheduled night of an evangelistic campaign, if you have the impression that the meeting should go on a night or two longer, invite all who have a similar impression to come to the front and take your hand. If any unsaved come, invite them to remain at the front to settle the matter now. If the unsaved do not come, ask if there are unsaved present who might make a favorable decision if the meetings were extended; if so, have them raise their hands. Unsaved people are often willing to do anything else except make a straightforward decision for Christ, but once they take one forward step, they obey the prompting of the Holy Spirit and take other forward steps.

49. *Present gifts to those who come forward.* Offer a booklet, calendar, or other article to all who will come to the front and take it. Explain that salvation is the gift of God freely offered to all who will accept it. Ask the unsaved to receive Christ at the same time they receive the gift you offer. One pastor had his own booklet on salvation which he gave to all who

would take it and promise to read it. The Christian
Business Men's Committee of Chicago gave away the
booklet, *Work that Wins* at all of their open-air meetings one summer. They would invite the unsaved to
remain behind for personal conference when they could
learn who they were.

50. *Extend the invitation at the close of the "white
gifts for the King" service.* A service called "White
Gifts for the King" leads into a good evangelistic invitation. At this service, people bring their gifts of
food, clothing, money and other things, to the front
of the church and put them on the communion table
or altar. This service is used most frequently at Christ-
mas and the gifts are for some missionary or benevolent
object. Emphasize the necessity of giving ourselves with
our gifts, and that the most acceptable gift to our King
is the gift of self (II Corinthians 8:5, Romans 12:1).
Invite those willing to give themselves to Christ and
take Him as personal Saviour and Lord to kneel at the
altar or stand in front.

51. *Urge the unsaved to prepare to meet loved ones
in heaven.* This invitation is very touching and should
be used carefully. An appeal such as this can be used
once during an evangelistic campaign, but only once.
This call may be directed to all who know they have
loved ones in heaven. First, ask those who know they
are prepared to meet those loved ones in heaven, to
come to the front. As they stand at the front, ask what
relatives they have in heaven — mother, father, sister,
brother, son, daughter. Then invite backsliders who
are not as ready as they once were, but are now ready
to rededicate themselves to Christ, to come. Next, in-

vite the unsaved—those who know they are not ready for heaven, but wish to be, and are ready to take the Saviour now. Emphasize that heaven is a prepared place for a prepared people, and that mere desire to go to heaven is not sufficient preparation; Christ must dwell in our hearts. The invitation hymn for this service may be "When the Roll Is Called Up Yonder," or "When the Saints Go Marching In." Rev. Arthur W. Littrell, of Warsaw, Indiana, has used this invitation effectively.

52. *Appeal to those who do not wish to die unsaved.* This appeal is directed to those who are not ready now to become Christians, but who do not intend to die in their sins; they mean to become Christians sometime before they are called to meet God. Ask any such in the audience to come up and take your hand and then return to their seats. If they take this step, they may wish to remain and seek the Lord. Dr. J. B. Cranfill, an honored Baptist writer of Dallas, Texas, but now with the Lord, responded to an invitation like this. In the *Western Recorder* of March 6, 1941, he tells of taking his girl friend to a brush arbor meeting one Sunday night when he was nearly eighteen years old. He says:

> We sat on the rear seat and listened attentively to the preacher's message. He was a very earnest man. His appeal to the lost brought many to the anxious seat, and in those good old days they had the mourners' bench, and one by one men and women came in response to the preacher's warnings and solicitations. Finally the preacher left off calling mourners and said:
> "I am impressed that within the sound of my voice there are some who, while not now seeking religion, mean sometime to seek Christ and become members of the church. If there is one here who ever intends at any time in his life to be a Christian, I want that one to come and give me his

hand as a token of that resolve."

I leaned over and asked the young lady in a subdued whisper if she was going. She shook her head. I said to her, "I must, to be honest with myself, go and give my hand, for I have always intended at some time to become a Christian."

With that I stepped forward into the aisle and made my way toward the minister. It was then that the miracle occurred. When I was about half way from my seat to where the preacher stood, there shone into my soul the light within. I saw myself as a lost and undone sinner, as one guilty in the sight of God and as a stranger to all the lofty things of life. God's Spirit had sought and found my spirit.

Yes, it was the light within. I did not know how to explain it then, nor do I know now. I was then nearly eighteen. I am now past eighty-two. The mystery remains and is not to be solved through any human mensuration or philosophy . . .

I didn't consciously lose the burden of my sins that night, but on the Wednesday night following, the burden disappeared and God's grace came singing into my soul, and through all the mutations of time since I first knew God, the love of Christ, which "passeth all understanding," has been with me.

Dr. Cranfill's experience illustrates the truth that God meets any soul that takes a step toward Him.

53. *Urge the skeptic to do the will of God and prove Him.* An appeal particularly applicable to the skeptical is based upon the challenge of Jesus in John 7:17, A.S.V., "If any man willeth to do his will, he shall know of the teaching, whether I speak from myself." Show that if there is any skepticism, infidelity, or doubt, these will melt away when one begins and continues to do the will of God. Challenge doubters and unbelievers to put God to the test by coming to the front and making themselves objects of prayer. Dr. B. H. Carroll, founder of Southwestern Baptist Theological Seminary, Fort

Worth, Texas, was won in this way. In one of the greatest sermons ever preached, entitled, "My Infidelity and What Became of It," [1] he tells the story of his conversion. He recites how he was baptized and joined the church as a boy, without any real conversion, and later drifted into skepticism and infidelity. He read widely from the books of both the Christian apologists and the infidels, but found no peace. He was discharged from the Confederate Army—crippled, poverty-stricken and in debt. He was bitter, discouraged and critical. He says:

I had sworn never to put my foot in another church. My father had died believing me lost. My mother—when does a mother give up a child?—came to me one day and begged, for her sake, that I would attend one more meeting. It was a Methodist camp meeting, held in the fall of 1865. I had not an atom of interest in it. I liked the singing, but the preaching did not touch me. But one day I shall never forget. It was Sunday at eleven o'clock. The great wooden shed was crowded. I stood on the outskirts, leaning on my crutches, wearily and somewhat scornfully enduring. The preacher made a failure even for him. There was nothing in his sermon. But when he came down, as I supposed to exhort as usual, he startled me not only by not exhorting, but by asking some questions that seemed meant for me.

He said: "You that stand aloof from Christianity and scorn us simple folks, what have you got? Answer honestly before God, have you found anything worth having where you are?" My heart answered in a moment: "Nothing under the whole heaven; absolutely nothing." As if he had heard my unspoken answer, he continued: "Is there anything else out there worth trying, that has any promise in it?" Again my heart answered: "Nothing; absolutely nothing. I have been to the jumping-off place on all these roads. They all lead to a bottomless abyss." "Well, then," he continued, "admitting there's nothing there, if there be a God, mustn't there be a something somewhere? If so, how do you know it is not

[1] *Sermons and Life Sketch of B. H. Carroll* by J. B. Cranfill (American Baptist Publication Society, Philadelphia, 1895, pp. 13-23).

here? Are you willing to test it? Have you the courage and fairness to try it? I don't ask you to read any book, nor study any evidences, nor make any difficult and tedious pilgrimages; that way is too long and time is too short. Are you willing to try it now; to make a practical, experimental test, you to be the judge of the result?"

These cool, calm and pertinent questions hit me with tremendous force, but I didn't understand the test. He continued: "I base my test on these two Scriptures: 'If any man willeth to do his will, he shall know of the teaching, whether it is of God'; 'Then shall we know, if we follow on to know the Lord.' "

For the first time I understood the import of these Scriptures. I had never before heard of such a translation for the first and had never examined the original text. In our version it says, "If any man will do his will, he shall know the doctrine, whether it be of God." But the preacher quoted it: "If any man willeth to do his will," showing that the knowledge as to whether the doctrine was of God depended not upon external action and not upon exact conformity with God's will, but upon the internal disposition—whosoever willeth or wishes to do God's will. The old translation seemed to make knowledge impossible; the new, practicable. In the second Scripture was also new light: "Then shall we know, if we follow on to know the Lord," which means that true knowledge follows persistence in the prosecution of it—that is, it comes not to temporary and spasmodic investigation.

So, when he invited all who were willing to make an immediate experimental test to come forward and give him their hands, I immediately went forward. I was not prepared for the stir which this action created. My infidelity and my hostile attitude toward Christianity were so well-known in the community that such action on my part developed quite a sensation. Some even began to shout. Whereupon, to prevent any misconception, I arose and stated that I was not converted; that perhaps they misunderstood what was meant by my coming forward; that my heart was as cold as ice; that my action meant no more than that I was willing to make an experimental test of the truth and power of the Christian religion; and that I was willing to persist in subjection to the test until a true solution could be found. This quieted matters.

The meeting closed without any change upon my part. The

last sermon had been preached, the benediction pronounced and the congregation was dispersing. A few ladies only remained, seated near the pulpit and engaged in singing. Feeling that the experiment was ended and the solution not found, I remained to hear them sing. As their last song, they sang:

> "O land of rest for thee I sigh;
> When will the moment come
> When I shall lay my armor by,
> And dwell in peace at home?"

The singing made a wonderful impression upon me. Its tones were as soft as the rustling of angels' wings. Suddenly there flashed upon my mind, like a light from heaven, this Scripture: "Come unto me, all ye that labour and are heavy laden, and I will give you rest." I did not see Jesus with my eyes, but I seemed to see Him standing before me, looking reproachfully and tenderly and pleadingly, seeming to rebuke me for having gone to all other sources for rest but the right one, and now inviting me to come to Him. In a moment I went, once and forever, casting myself unreservedly and for all time at Christ's feet, and in a moment the rest came, indescribable and unspeakable, and it has remained from that day until now.

It is doubtful that Dr. Carroll could have been moved in any other way. He knew the Bible, and he knew the arguments for and against Christianity. This practical appeal to begin doing something rather than trying to understand, met his need.

I. Combination, or Progressive, Invitations

In this classification we give the invitations which combine two or more of the foregoing methods. Some of the best soul-winners prefer the progressive type of invitation which leads people in easy steps into a full committal.

54. *Invite those who desire spiritual advice to raise their hands and come forward for instruction.* While all heads are bowed, ask all who feel the need of Jesus, or are concerned about their souls, to raise their hands for

prayer. Pray for them. Announce an invitation hymn, and invite them to the front for further instruction. Avoid giving the impression of deception in the use of this invitation. Do not demand that those who raised their hands come to the front, and do not send personal workers to plead with them, or they will feel that they have been trapped. Personal workers or friends may offer to accompany them to the front, but pressure should not be used. Explain the need of going through to complete victory and assurance. Assure them that you will not take unfair advantage of them if they come to the front. Urge them kindly but firmly to come forward for entire committal and further conference. This is the plan of salvation used more than any other at Victory Center in Chicago. The Christian Business Men's Committee, an international group, operates Victory Center as a permanent evangelistic station in the heart of the Loop in Chicago. This committee holds and broadcasts an evangelistic meeting every noon five days a week in this location. The leading evangelistic preachers of America and the world conduct the evangelistic services at this center. Mr. Frank Sheriff, chairman of the committee, often conducts the invitation, and he prefers this progressive plan.

55. *Employ Dr. Gage's decision day invitation.* Dr. Albert H. Gage suggests an excellent invitation for a decision day service in his book, *Evangelism of Youth,* chapter seven. He advises careful preparation for the decision day by both teachers and officers. They should survey each class, interview every scholar if possible, pray for every unsaved scholar by name and seek a one hundred per cent attendance.

On decision day, the entire Sunday school above the age of eleven should meet together, while the juniors meet in another room. The speaker should use the story of the call of Samuel and show how God speaks to boys and girls. Explain how God calls people today to accept salvation and become Christians. Tell how to receive a gift by some object lesson demonstration. Show how the first step in the Christian life is to receive God's gift of love, the Lord Jesus Christ, as Saviour and Lord. Call for a season of silent prayer. Have eight or ten respected Christians, ranging in age from the oldest Christian in the church to the youngest, step to the front and give their testimonies, saying when God called them, whether or not they are glad to be Christians, and whether or not they can recommend Christ to others. Ask for perfect quiet in the room as all bow their heads in silent prayer listening for God's voice. Those who gave testimonies remain in front while the invitation goes out. As the spirit of prayer and quietness reigns, ask those who know God is calling them to the Christian life, to arise and come to the front and stand with the others already there. Take plenty of time for this part of the service. Quite a little time may elapse before anyone comes, but do not be disturbed. Remain quiet and let God speak. When the movement starts, they will come one by one at first, then in two's and three's, and sometimes in whole sections. Tell them not to come because others are coming, or because you wish them to come, but because God speaks to them and tells them to come.

After this part of the invitation ends, sing an invitation hymn, and invite older people to come to confess Christ and to unite with the church.

The writer has used this invitation more than once when so many came that it was impossible to deal with them individually. In that case, take them all into another room, and ask some of the deacons and teachers to come along. Again explain the way of salvation with the utmost simplicity and clarity. Repeat the prayer of committal which you will ask them all to pray, each one to pray it honestly and earnestly as his own prayer. Then have them kneel and pray in unison as you direct. Give them a few words of the prayer and wait until they have prayed those words, then give the next few words, and so on until you reach the "Amen," after which you ask every one to be seated. The prayer of committal can be phrased as follows: "Lord Jesus, I am a sinner, lost and perishing, but I come to Thee. I now receive Thee as my personal Saviour and Lord. Save me from all sin, make me Thy child, give me eternal life, write my name in Thy book of life, and receive me into Thy kingdom. Help me to confess Thee before men, and to love Thee and serve Thee as long as I live. Thank Thee, Lord, for hearing and answering my prayer, for Jesus' sake. Amen."

After the group has been seated, ask a few questions as follows: "How many of you prayed that prayer and meant it? Put up your hands. Do you believe God heard your prayer? If God heard it, did He answer? If God heard and answered your prayer, what does that mean? If you know you are now saved, lift your hand." Take the name and address of every person who has made a decision and give them all the personal help possible from that time forward. Do not press the matter of baptism and church membership too rapidly.

Confer with the parents of children before baptizing their children or receiving them into church membership.

56. *Employ Dr. Taylor's plan for decision day.* If anyone fears that Dr. Gage's plan might create too much of a mass movement, we suggest the method outlined by Dr. Frederick E. Taylor, formerly pastor of the First Baptist Church, Indianapolis. Dr. Taylor produced an excellent book entitled *The Evangelistic Church,* in which he recommends a plan for decision day in the Bible school. He also counsels careful preparation with much prayer. On decision day the lesson is omitted, and the pastor brings a short message to the whole school on why and how to become a Christian. Without any invitation, the assembly is dismissed, and the teachers take their classes to their respective rooms. Those who are Christians have been instructed beforehand to pray for those who are not. The teacher opens the class with prayer and asks those who are not Christians to receive Christ. The teacher can deal with the pupils personally if necessary. At the bell, the school reassembles, and the pastor takes charge. He asks those who have told their teachers that they would become Christians, to stand. Then he calls upon others to stand as an indica-tion that they now wish to become Christians. The value of this plan is that the teachers have the privilege of winning their own pupils to Christ. Those who have made commitments receive personal calls during the week, and are further instructed.

57. *Employ Dr. Pierce's chart.* Dr. Earle V. Pierce, of Minneapolis, says that, during his earlier ministry, he sometimes had a chart put on the platform, showing

forward steps for Christians. The items on this chart
would be somewhat as follows:

1. Receive Christ as Saviour and Lord;
2. Be baptized and unite with the church;
3. Set up a family altar;
4. Read the Bible daily;
5. Become a tither;
6. Seek to win souls by personal witnessing;
7. Subscribe to the church paper.

Dr. Pierce framed his invitations to include these various
steps. He kept the chart before the people all through
a campaign, and sought to commit every person to as
many steps as possible.

58. *Present an exhortation supporting the invitation.*
In the early days of our country, particularly in the
Methodist movement, churches had "exhorters." These
"exhorters" were not preachers, but were laymen who
could speak fluently and effectively in public meetings.
After the preacher's invitation, the "exhorters" would
often take over and exhort the sinners to flee from the
wrath to come. Some of these "exhorters" could make
a powerful evangelistic appeal, and often turned many
to the Lord.

We can still use the same principle on occasion.
When the invitation apparently is a failure, have the
people sit down, and ask some of the saints who have
a burden for souls to speak. The Holy Spirit may take
hold of the testimony of some humble Christian and
use it to melt the coldness of an audience and turn
sinners to repentance. Renew the invitation if the spiritual atmosphere seems to change after some of the
Christians have exhorted. One of the most impressive
demonstrations of the Holy Spirit's working that the

author ever saw came about one Sunday night when this suggestion was used.

59. *Eliminate the sermon.* During times of genuine revival, unusual procedures may be justified. Occasions may arise when the Holy Spirit is so powerfully at work that sermons are needless. The Spirit can move people through a hymn, a solo, a prayer, or a testimony. If such a thing occurs before the sermon has been given, it would be better to stop right there and give the invitation. Sermons can wait if souls will come to Christ without them. In such a case, a longer invitation could be given, and more time devoted to helping seekers. If the Spirit of God is at work and souls are being saved, people will not mind if services do not follow the usual order.

60. *Utilize Dr. Joshua's invitation.* Dr. Peter R. Joshua, a Presbyterian minister, tells of an invitation given down underneath the earth in a Welsh coal mine. One of the miners called the men together in a large underground room and asked them to put out their lights while he spoke to them. In the inky-black darkness of the mine, this Christian man spoke plainly and pointedly to his fellows about Christ and urged them to receive Him. He asked all who were willing to receive the Lord Jesus Christ to light their lamps. This act would indicate that they were coming to the Light of the World, and would follow Him, and let their lights shine for Him henceforth. Lights began to go on here and there until many were burning. Dr. Joshua says it was a most inspiring sight. Dr. Joshua frequently tells this story vividly and dramatically preparatory to an invitation. He asks people to come to the Light

of the World and shine for Christ, and to indicate this by standing.

61. *Employ slide and film invitations.* A promising field of evangelistic methodology lies in the realm of the screen. Many sets of lantern slides deal with Biblical and evangelistic subjects, and can very appropriately lead to an invitation. A personal appeal should follow the pictures, but the invitation hymn will be more effective if also thrown upon the screen. Some people will come forward a little more readily with the room in semidarkness than they will after all the bright lights are flooding the room. There are many dealers in slides in various parts of the country. Standard slides are made of glass, but many slides are now made of film, and these latter are lighter and more compact. The Bond Slide Company, 68 West Washington Street, Chicago, Illinois, is one of the few producers of lantern slides. They are also dealers and handle practically everything in the way of slides. The cartoons of Dr. E. J. Pace have been put on slides and make very good evangelistic material. These Pace slides come in sets of thirty-five or forty, but that number is almost too many to use in one message. Some of the missions use only one slide, and have it on the screen while the whole message is given.

Another venture in this field is the talking moving picture film. Here is a modern invention that will doubtless be used widely in evangelism in the days ahead. The Scripture Visualized Institute, 325 West Huron Street, Chicago, Illinois, produces the C. O. Baptista films. These films are all-talking. They are Scripturally sound and carry a strong evangelistic emphasis. This company receives many reports of spiritual quickening and conversion through the use of their films. A picture four hundred feet long requires ten minutes to run, while one of twelve hundred feet takes thirty minutes. The invitation is usually given after the picture. If the picture is only ten or fifteen minutes long, then an evangelistic message of about the same length is necessary in order to lead into the invitation. The same methods of invitation can be used with these films as would be used with evangelistic sermons.

The Moody Bible Institute of Chicago has a color picture in sound entitled "They Live Forever." The picture requires approximately fifty minutes. Lieutenant Whittaker and Sergeant Bartek give their testimonies in this picture, and the evangelistic appeal is strong. The Institute has received reports of many conversions through the use of this film.

J. PERSONALIZED INVITATIONS

On rare occasions it is permissible to approach people personally during an invitation. Usually we should refrain from doing personal work with anyone during the invitation. One reason why some people stay away from evangelistic meetings is that they do not wish to be solicited personally. One of our leading evangelists makes it a point to allow no personal work while he is giving the invitation. He announces to his audience that people can bring their friends without any fear that they will be embarrassed by personal workers. He says that some people come to his services simply because they know that no one will make a personal approach to them. This evangelist says that sinners will respond to the invitation without the personal approach once sufficient conviction grips them.

However, many people have yielded to the personal appeal during the invitation and have been genuinely converted. When the Holy Spirit is working in power, and Christians become deeply concerned about the lost, then personal work during the invitation seems to be natural. Christians find it hard to restrain themselves from personal work when revivals reach a white heat. Therefore, this writer believes that a hard and fast rule against personal work during the invitation is wrong. Christians should make certain their lives are right, and that the Holy Spirit is prompting them, before they deal with individuals personally during the invitation. Even then, it is doubtful that there should be much persuasion and pleading.

Some men have used the personalized appeal with success, and we are giving a few examples of this invitation

62. *Ask Christians to shake hands with the unsaved.* As a variation in invitation procedure, ask the Christians to go to any unsaved persons in the house for whose salvation they are praying, and shake hands with them. Sing the invitation hymn, "I Am Praying For You." Tell the Christians that they are not to say anything, but merely to shake hands with any unsaved persons in the place for whom they are praying. Explain to the unsaved that you do not wish to embarrass them, but do wish them to know how much concern there is for them. Benefit will come to Christians as they go to the unsaved and grasp their hands, and some Christians will venture to say a word of invitation. Often a whole

line of Christians will go to the same unsaved person. The unsaved may be surprised to know how many people are praying for them. Another thing about this plan is that it arouses Christians to a keener sense of their responsibility for the lost. After a saint has shaken a sinner's hand in a service like this, he feels that he must keep on praying for him, and pray harder than ever. We have seen some sinners shed tears and tremble as the Christians came by to shake their hands.

63. *Motion to the unsaved to come forward.* While giving the invitation, the experienced evangelist may be able to catch the eye of some person under conviction. If he can catch this person's attention for a moment or two, and motion to him with his forefinger, he may be able to induce him to come. Care should be taken to shield the movement so only the person receiving the signal knows what is meant. Dr. J. C. Massee says he has been able to bring many an unsaved person out of his seat to the front by this simple device.

64. *Walk through the aisles and clasp the hands of the unsaved.* Dr. S. J. Reid, formerly the pastor of Tabernacle Baptist Church in Chicago, says that he has often walked up and down the aisles with his hand outstretched, inviting the unsaved to reach out and take him by the hand as a sign they wish to be saved. Because it is so customary and natural to take an extended hand, the unsaved person may find this the easiest way to make the first movement toward God. The evangelist can quote Romans 10:21, "But to Israel he saith, All day long have I stretched forth my hands unto a disobedient and gainsaying people," and ask them to take God's hand as they take his.

65. *Address an individual.* The most personalized method the writer has ever seen was used from time to time by a rescue mission superintendent in Chicago. This preacher would pick out some man in the audience and appeal to him personally from the pulpit to leave his seat and come to the front to accept Jesus Christ. The appeal might be something like this: "That man with the brown coat and bald head in the fourth row, will you come up and receive Christ as your Saviour? Yes, I mean you there looking at me now. You are not happy, are you? Shake your head if you are not. No, of course you are not. I can see the marks of sin and sadness written on your face. Jesus Christ died for you because He loved you. He lives on high right now, and will save you and give you peace and happiness if you will let Him into your heart. You need Jesus. You want to do it, don't you? Yes, of course you do. Come on, do it now. You will never regret it. The world hasn't anything more to offer you, but Jesus offers you everything you need. Yes, I am talking to you directly, but the Holy Spirit is pleading with you more than I ever could. Get up and come, friend. I will meet you halfway. Let's do it. Come now. Thank God, he is coming! Who else will come with him?" Probably this method could be used only in a mission service, and should be used with caution even there.

* * *

Reader, we have outlined sixty-five ways to give evangelistic invitations. Probably you can add other methods to this compilation; we hope so. This book certainly does not include every possible way of giving the evangelistic appeal, but we have included everything that seemed to us worth mentioning. Our highest hope is that you will be able to win more souls by using some of the suggestions in this book. Nothing else matters. Take the methods that appeal to you and use them. But do not rely upon mere methods alone: depend upon the Holy Spirit and the Word of God, and use any methods the Spirit may suggest. We need more good evangelists today. We need more evangelistic pastors. "Do the work of an evangelist" (II Timothy 4:5).

6

APPENDIX A

SCRIPTURE QUOTATIONS FOR USE IN GIVING INVITATIONS

QUOTATIONS from the Word of God have peculiar power to arrest attention and to drive home divine truths. A few well-chosen Scriptural quotations will make an invitation more forceful and gripping. God has promised to bless His Word, and we should make frequent use of it. Note the following passages as to the energy of the divine Word:

So shall my word be that goeth forth out of my mouth: it shall not return unto me void, but it shall accomplish that which I please, and it shall prosper in the thing whereto I sent it (Isaiah 55:11).

Is not my word like as a fire? saith the Lord; and like a hammer that breaketh the rock in pieces? (Jeremiah 23:29).

It is the spirit that quickeneth; the flesh profiteth nothing: the words that I speak unto you, they are spirit, and they are life (John 6:63).

And take the helmet of salvation, and the sword of the Spirit, which is the word of God (Ephesians 6:17).

For the word of God is quick, and powerful, and sharper than any twoedged sword, piercing even to the dividing asunder of soul and spirit, and of the joints and marrow, and is a discerner of the thoughts and intents of the heart (Hebrews 4:12).

Being born again, not of corruptible seed, but of incorruptible, by the word of God, which liveth and abideth for ever (I Peter 1:23).

Of his own will begat he us with the word of truth, that we should be a kind of firstfruits of his creatures (James 1:18).

Wherefore lay apart all filthiness and superfluity of naughtiness, and receive with meekness the engrafted word, which is able to save your souls (James 1:21).

Dr. Oscar Lowry used to insist that ministers should fill their sermons with Scripture quotations as a means of insuring the blessing of God upon the message. He claimed that the Word should be quoted exactly and the references given, and his own ministry was a remarkable demonstration of this practice. Dr. Lowry was a great evangelist and has written a most helpful book entitled, *Scripture Memorizing for Successful Soul-Winning*.

We give the Scripture quotations which follow as valuable both in evangelistic invitations and as texts for evangelistic sermons.

I. QUOTATIONS FROM THE OLD TESTAMENT

. . . and when I see the blood, I will pass over you (Exodus 12:13).

. . . Who is on the Lord's side? let him come unto me (Exodus 32:26).

. . . for it is the blood that maketh an atonement for the soul (Leviticus 17:11).

. . . come thou with us, and we will do thee good: for the Lord hath spoken good concerning Israel (Numbers 10:29).

. . . and be sure your sin will find you out (Numbers 32:23).

I call heaven and earth to record this day against you, that I have set before you life and death, blessing and cursing: therefore choose life, that both thou and thy seed may live (Deuteronomy 30:19).

. . . choose you this day whom ye will serve . . . but as for me and my house, we will serve the Lord (Joshua 24:15).

. . . for the Lord seeth not as man seeth; for man looketh on the outward appearance, but the Lord looketh on the heart (I Samuel 16:7).

If my people, which are called by my name, shall humble themselves, and pray, and seek my face, and turn from their wicked ways; then will I hear from heaven, and will forgive their sin, and will heal their land (II Chronicles 7:14).

. . . The Lord is with you, while ye be with him; and if ye seek him, he will be found of you; but if ye forsake him, he will forsake you (II Chronicles 15:2).

Kiss the Son, lest he be angry, and ye perish from the way, when his wrath is kindled but a little. Blessed are all they that put their trust in him (Psalm 2:12).

They that sow in tears shall reap in joy. He that goeth forth and weepeth, bearing precious seed, shall doubtless come again with rejoicing, bringing his sheaves with him (Psalm 126:5-6).

For the backsliding of the simple shall slay them, and the careless ease of fools shall destroy them (Proverbs 1:32, A.S.V.).

There is a way which seemeth right unto a man, but the end thereof are the ways of death (Proverbs 14:12).

My son, give me thine heart . . . (Proverbs 23:26).

Boast not thyself of to morrow; for thou knowest not what a day may bring forth (Proverbs 27:1).

He that covereth his sins shall not prosper; but whoso confesseth and forsaketh them shall have mercy (Proverbs 28:13).

He, that being often reproved hardeneth his neck, shall suddenly be destroyed, and that without remedy (Proverbs 29:1).

Remember now thy Creator in the days of thy youth, while the evil days come not, nor the years draw nigh, when thou shalt say, I have no pleasure in them (Ecclesiastes 12:1).

Come now, and let us reason together, saith the Lord: though your sins be as scarlet, they shall be as white as snow; though they be red like crimson, they shall be as wool (Isaiah 1:18).

I have blotted out, as a thick cloud, thy transgressions, and, as a cloud, thy sins: return unto me; for I have redeemed thee (Isaiah 44:22).

Look unto me, and be ye saved, all the ends of the earth: for I am God, and there is none else (Isaiah 45:22).

(This text was used when Charles Haddon Spurgeon was converted.)

But he was wounded for our transgressions, he was bruised for our iniquities: the chastisement of our peace was upon him; and with his stripes we are healed. All we like sheep have gone astray; we have turned every one to his own way; and the Lord hath laid on him the iniquity of us all (Isaiah 53:5-6).

Ho, every one that thirsteth, come ye to the waters, and he that hath no money; come ye, buy, and eat; yea, come, buy wine and milk without money and without price (Isaiah 55:1).

Seek ye the Lord while he may be found, call ye upon him while he is near: let the wicked forsake his way, and the unrighteous man his thoughts: and let him return unto the Lord, and he will have mercy upon him; and to our God, for he will abundantly pardon (Isaiah 55:6-7).

But the wicked are like the troubled sea, when it cannot rest, whose waters cast up mire and dirt. There is no peace, saith my God, to the wicked (Isaiah 57:20-21).

Behold, the Lord's hand is not shortened, that it cannot save; neither his ear heavy, that it cannot hear: but your iniquities have separated between you and your God, and your sins have hid his face from you, that he will not hear (Isaiah 59:1-2).

For my people have committed two evils; they have forsaken me the fountain of living waters, and hewed them out cisterns, broken cisterns, that can hold no water (Jeremiah 2:13).

Thine own wickedness shall correct thee, and thy backslidings shall reprove thee: know therefore and see that it is an evil thing and bitter, that thou hast forsaken the Lord thy God, and that my fear is not in thee, saith the Lord God of hosts (Jeremiah 2:19).

For though thou wash thee with nitre [lye, A.S.V.], and take thee much soap, yet thine iniquity is marked before me, saith the Lord God (Jeremiah 2:22).

Turn, O backsliding children, saith the Lord; for I am married unto you: and I will take you one of a city, and two of a family, and I will bring you to Zion (Jeremiah 3:14).

Return, ye backsliding children, and I will heal your backslidings. Behold, we come unto thee; for thou art the Lord our God (Jeremiah 3:22).

. . . Break up your fallow ground, and sow not among thorns. Circumcise yourselves to the Lord, and take away the foreskins of your heart, ye men of Judah and inhabitants of Jerusalem: lest my fury come forth like fire, and burn that none can quench it, because of the evil of your doings (Jeremiah 4:3-4).

Thus saith the Lord, Stand ye in the ways, and see, and ask for the old paths, where is the good way, and walk therein, and ye shall find rest for your souls. But they said, We will not walk therein (Jeremiah 6:16).

The harvest is past, the summer is ended, and we are not saved (Jeremiah 8:20).

Can the Ethiopian change his skin, or the leopard his spots? then may ye also do good, that are accustomed to do evil (Jeremiah 13:23).

The heart is deceitful above all things, and desperately wicked: who can know it? (Jeremiah 17:9).

And ye shall seek me, and find me, when ye shall search for me with all your heart. And I will be found of you, saith the Lord . . . (Jeremiah 29:13-14).

Let us search and try our ways, and turn again to the Lord. Let us lift up our heart with our hands unto God in the heavens (Lamentations 3:40-41).

Turn thou us unto thee, O Lord, and we shall be turned; renew our days as of old (Lamentations 5:21).

The soul that sinneth, it shall die (Ezekiel 18:4, 20).

Have I any pleasure at all that the wicked should die? saith the Lord God: and not that he should return from his ways, and live? (Ezekiel 18:23).

Cast away from you all your transgressions, whereby ye have transgressed; and make you a new heart and a new spirit: for why will ye die, O house of Israel? For I have no pleasure in the death of him that dieth, saith the Lord God: wherefore turn yourselves, and live ye (Ezekiel 18:31-32).

Say unto them, As I live, saith the Lord God, I have no pleasure in the death of the wicked; but that the wicked turn from his way and live: turn ye, turn ye from your evil ways; for why will ye die, O house of Israel? (Ezekiel 33:11).

TEKEL; Thou art weighed in the balances, and art found wanting (Daniel 5:27).

Sow to yourselves in righteousness, reap in mercy; break up your fallow ground: for it is time to seek the Lord, till he come and rain righteousness upon you (Hosea 10:12).

Therefore also now, saith the Lord, turn ye even to me with all your heart, and with fasting, and with weeping, and with mourning: and rend your heart, and not your garments, and turn unto the Lord your God: for he is gracious and merciful, slow to anger, and of great kindness, and repenteth him of the evil (Joel 2:12-13).

Woe to them that are at ease in Zion, and to them that are secure in the mountain of Samaria . . . (Amos 6:1, A.S.V.).

The Lord is slow to anger, and great in power, and will not at all acquit the wicked . . . (Nahum 1:3).

. . . the just shall live by his faith (Habakkuk 2:4).

. . . O Lord, revive thy work in the midst of the years, in the midst of the years make known; in wrath remember mercy (Habakkuk 3:2).

Therefore say thou unto them, Thus saith the Lord of hosts; Turn ye unto me, saith the Lord of hosts, and I will turn unto you, saith the Lord of hosts (Zechariah 1:3).

. . . Not by might, nor by power, but by my spirit, saith the Lord of hosts (Zechariah 4:6).

But who may abide the day of his coming? and who shall stand when he appeareth? for he is like a refiner's fire, and like fullers' soap: and he shall sit as a refiner and purifier of silver . . . (Malachi 3:2-3).

. . . Return unto me, and I will return unto you, saith the Lord of hosts . . . (Malachi 3:7).

II. QUOTATIONS FROM THE NEW TESTAMENT

But seek ye first the kingdom of God, and his righteousness; and all these things shall be added unto you (Matthew 6:33).

Enter ye in at the strait gate: for wide is the gate, and broad is the way, that leadeth to destruction, and many there be which go in thereat: because strait is the gate, and narrow is the way, which leadeth unto life, and few there be that find it (Matthew 7:13-14).

Not every one that saith unto me, Lord, Lord, shall enter into the kingdom of heaven; but he that doeth the will of my Father which is in heaven (Matthew 7:21).

Whosoever therefore shall confess me before men, him will I confess also before my Father which is in heaven. But whosoever shall deny me before men, him will I also deny before my Father which is in heaven (Matthew 10:32-33).

Come unto me, all ye that labour and are heavy laden, and I will give you rest. Take my yoke upon you, and learn of me;

for I am meek and lowly in heart: and ye shall find rest unto your souls. For my yoke is easy, and my burden is light (Matthew 11:28-30).

He that is not with me is against me; and he that gathereth not with me scattereth abroad (Matthew 12:30).

. . . Verily I say unto you, Except ye be converted, and become as little children, ye shall not enter into the kingdom of heaven (Matthew 18:3).

Therefore be ye also ready: for in such an hour as ye think not the Son of man cometh (Matthew 24:44).

For what shall it profit a man, if he shall gain the whole world, and lose his own soul? (Mark 8:36).

Whosoever therefore shall be ashamed of me and of my words in this adulterous and sinful generation; of him also shall the Son of man be ashamed, when he cometh in the glory of his Father with the holy angels (Mark 8:38).

. . . Suffer the little children to come unto me, and forbid them not: for of such is the kingdom of God (Mark 10:14).

He that believeth and is baptized shall be saved; but he that believeth not shall be damned (Mark 16:16).

. . . Follow me (Luke 5:27).

I came not to call the righteous, but sinners to repentance (Luke 5:32).

And why call ye me, Lord, Lord, and do not the things which I say? (Luke 6:46).

. . . No man, having put his hand to the plough, and looking back, is fit for the kingdom of God (Luke 9:62).

. . . The harvest truly is great, but the labourers are few: pray ye therefore the Lord of the harvest, that he would send forth labourers into his harvest (Luke 10:2).

But God said unto him, Thou fool, this night thy soul shall be required of thee: then whose shall those things be, which thou hast provided? (Luke 12:20).

I tell you, Nay: but, except ye repent, ye shall all likewise perish (Luke 13:3, 5).

I say unto you, that likewise joy shall be in heaven over one sinner that repenteth, more than over ninety and nine just persons, which need no repentance (Luke 15:7).

No servant can serve two masters: for either he will hate

the one, and love the other; or else he will hold to the one, and despise the other. Ye cannot serve God and mammon (Luke 16:13).

Remember Lot's wife (Luke 17:32).

For the Son of man is come to seek and to save that which was lost (Luke 19:10).

. . . What is this then that is written, The stone which the builders rejected, the same is become the head of the corner? Whosoever shall fall upon that stone shall be broken; but on whomsoever it shall fall, it will grind him to powder (Luke 20:17-18).

Watch ye therefore, and pray always, that ye may be accounted worthy to escape all these things that shall come to pass, and to stand before the Son of man (Luke 21:36).

He came unto his own, and his own received him not. But as many as received him, to them gave he power to become the sons of God, even to them that believe on his name (John 1:11-12).

. . . Verily, verily, I say unto thee, Except a man be born again, he cannot see the kingdom of God (John 3:3).

Verily, verily, I say unto thee, Except a man be born of water and of the Spirit, he cannot enter into the kingdom of God. That which is born of the flesh is flesh; and that which is born of the Spirit is spirit (John 3:5-6).

John 3:14-19 is the greatest salvation passage in the Bible, and it may be quoted in whole or in part with great effect. Verse 18 is especially suited to induce faith.

14 And as Moses lifted up the serpent in the wilderness, even so must the Son of man be lifted up:

15 That whosoever believeth in him should not perish, but have eternal life.

16 For God so loved the world, that he gave his only begotten Son, that whosoever believeth in him should not perish, but have everlasting life.

17 For God sent not his Son into the world to condemn the world; but that the world through him might be saved.

18 He that believeth on him is not condemned: but he that believeth not is condemned already, because he hath not believed in the name of the only begotten Son of God.

19 And this is the condemnation, that light is come into the world, and men loved darkness rather than light, because their deeds were evil.

He that believeth on the Son hath everlasting life: and he that believeth not the Son shall not see life; but the wrath of God abideth on him (John 3:36).

. . . If thou knewest the gift of God, and who it is that saith to thee, Give me to drink; thou wouldest have asked of him, and he would have given thee living water (John 4:10).

Verily, verily, I say unto you, He that heareth my word, and believeth on him that sent me, hath everlasting life, and shall not come into condemnation; but is passed from death unto life (John 5:24).

. . . This is the work of God, that ye believe on him whom he hath sent (John 6:29).

All that the Father giveth me shall come to me; and him that cometh to me I will in no wise cast out (John 6:37).

If any man willeth to do his will, he shall know of the teaching, whether it is of God, or whether I speak from myself (John 7:17, A.S.V.).

I am the light of the world: he that followeth me shall not walk in darkness, but shall have the light of life (John 8:12).

I said therefore unto you, that ye shall die in your sins: for if ye believe not that I am he, ye shall die in your sins (John 8:24).

If the Son therefore shall make you free, ye shall be free indeed (John 8:36).

I am the door: by me if any man enter in, he shall be saved, and shall go in and out, and find pasture (John 10:9).

. . . I am come that they might have life, and that they might have it more abundantly (John 10:10).

And I give unto them eternal life; and they shall never perish, neither shall any man pluck them out of my hand. My Father, which gave them me, is greater than all; and no man is able to pluck them out of my Father's hand (John 10:28-29).

. . . I am the resurrection, and the life: he that believeth in me, though he were dead, yet shall he live: and whosoever liveth and believeth in me shall never die. Believest thou this? (John 11:25-26).

And I, if I be lifted up from the earth, will draw all men unto me (John 12:32).

. . . I am the way, the truth, and the life: no man cometh unto the Father, but by me (John 14:6).

Peace I leave with you, my peace I give unto you: not as the world giveth, give I unto you. Let not your heart be troubled, neither let it be afraid (John 14:27).

And this is life eternal, that they might know thee the only true God, and Jesus Christ, whom thou hast sent (John 17:3).

But ye shall receive power, after that the Holy Ghost is come upon you: and ye shall be witnesses unto me both in Jerusalem, and in all Judaea, and in Samaria, and unto the uttermost part of the earth (Acts 1:8).

Then Peter said unto them, Repent, and be baptized every one of you in the name of Jesus Christ for the remission of sins, and ye shall receive the gift of the Holy Ghost (Acts 2:38).

Repent ye therefore, and be converted, that your sins may be blotted out, when the times of refreshing shall come from the presence of the Lord (Acts 3:19).

Neither is there salvation in any other: for there is none other name under heaven given among men, whereby we must be saved (Acts 4:12).

Be it known unto you therefore, men and brethren, that through this man is preached unto you the forgiveness of sins: and by him all that believe are justified from all things, from which ye could not be justified by the law of Moses (Acts 13:38-39).

And they said, Believe on the Lord Jesus Christ, and thou shalt be saved, and thy house (Acts 16:31).

The times of ignorance therefore God overlooked; but now he commandeth men that they should all everywhere repent (Acts 17:30, A.S.V.).

And now why tarriest thou? arise, and be baptized, and wash away thy sins, calling on the name of the Lord (Acts 22:16).

And Paul said, I would to God, that not only thou, but also all that hear me this day, were both almost, and altogether such as I am, except these bonds (Acts 26:29).

Therefore thou art inexcusable, O man, whosoever thou art that judgest: for wherein thou judgest another, thou condemnest thyself; for thou that judgest doest the same things (Romans 2:1).

Or despisest thou the riches of his goodness and forbearance and longsuffering; not knowing that the goodness of God leadeth thee to repentance? (Romans 2:4).

For all have sinned, and come short of the glory of God (Romans 3:23).

Likewise reckon ye also yourselves to be dead indeed unto sin, but alive unto God through Jesus Christ our Lord (Romans 6:11).

Know ye not, that to whom ye yield yourselves servants to obey, his servants ye are to whom ye obey; whether of sin unto death, or of obedience unto righteousness? (Romans 6:16).

For the wages of sin is death; but the gift of God is eternal life through Jesus Christ our Lord (Romans 6:23).

So then they that are in the flesh cannot please God (Romans 8:8).

For they being ignorant of God's righteousness, and going about to establish their own righteousness, have not submitted themselves unto the righteousness of God. For Christ is the end of the law for righteousness to every one that believeth (Romans 10:3-4).

That if thou shalt confess with thy mouth the Lord Jesus, and shalt believe in thine heart that God hath raised him from the dead, thou shalt be saved. For with the heart man believeth unto righteousness; and with the mouth confession is made unto salvation (Romans 10:9-10).

For whosoever shall call upon the name of the Lord shall be saved (Romans 10:13).

I beseech you therefore, brethren, by the mercies of God, that ye present your bodies a living sacrifice, holy, acceptable unto God, which is your reasonable service. And be not conformed to this world: but be ye transformed by the renewing of your mind, that ye may prove what is that good, and acceptable, and perfect, will of God (Romans 12:1-2).

And that, knowing the time, that now it is high time to awake out of sleep: for now is our salvation nearer than when we believed. The night is far spent, the day is at hand: let us therefore cast off the works of darkness, and let us put on the armour of light (Romans 13:11-12).

So then every one of us shall give account of himself to God (Romans 14:12).

Know ye not that the unrighteous shall not inherit the kingdom of God? Be not deceived: neither fornicators, nor idolaters, nor adulterers, nor effeminate, nor abusers of themselves with mankind, nor thieves, nor covetous, nor drunkards, nor revilers, nor extortioners, shall inherit the kingdom of God. And such were some of you: but ye are washed, but ye are sanctified, but ye are justified in the name of the Lord Jesus, and by the Spirit of our God (I Corinthians 6:9-11).

What? know ye not that your body is the temple of the Holy Ghost which is in you, which ye have of God, and ye are not your own? For ye are bought with a price: therefore glorify God in your body, and in your spirit, which are God's (I Corinthians 6:19-20).

But take heed lest by any means this liberty of your's become a stumblingblock to them that are weak (I Corinthians 8:9).

There hath no temptation taken you but such as is common to man: but God is faithful, who will not suffer you to be tempted above that ye are able; but will with the temptation also make a way to escape, that ye may be able to bear it (I Corinthians 10:13).

But if our gospel be hid, it is hid to them that are lost: in whom the god of this world hath blinded the minds of them which believe not, lest the light of the glorious gospel of Christ, who is the image of God, should shine unto them (II Corinthians 4:3-4).

For we must all appear before the judgment seat of Christ; that every one may receive the things done in his body, according to that he hath done, whether it be good or bad (II Corinthians 5:10).

Now then we are ambassadors for Christ, as though God did beseech you by us: we pray you in Christ's stead, be ye reconciled to God. For he hath made him to be sin for us, who knew no sin; that we might be made the righteousness of God in him (II Corinthians 5:20-21).

. . . behold, now is the accepted time; behold, now is the day of salvation (II Corinthians 6:2).

Wherefore come out from among them, and be ye separate, saith the Lord, and touch not the unclean thing; and I will receive you, and will be a Father unto you, and ye shall be my sons and daughters, saith the Lord Almighty (II Corinthians 6:17-18).

For ye know the grace of our Lord Jesus Christ, that, though he was rich, yet for your sakes he became poor, that ye through his poverty might be rich (II Corinthians 8:9).

Thanks be unto God for his unspeakable gift (II Corinthians 9:15).

And he said unto me, My grace is sufficient for thee: for my strength is made perfect in weakness . . . (II Corinthians 12:9).

Examine yourselves, whether ye be in the faith; prove your own selves. Know ye not your own selves, how that Jesus Christ is in you, except ye be reprobates? (II Corinthians 13:5).

For as many as are of the works of the law are under the curse: for it is written, Cursed is every one that continueth not in all things which are written in the book of the law to do them (Galatians 3:10).

Christ hath redeemed us from the curse of the law, being made a curse for us: for it is written, Cursed is every one that hangeth on a tree (Galatians 3:13).

Be not deceived; God is not mocked: for whatsoever a man soweth, that shall he also reap (Galatians 6:7).

For by grace are ye saved through faith; and that not of yourselves: it is the gift of God: not of works, lest any man should boast (Ephesians 2:8-9).

And grieve not the holy Spirit of God, whereby ye are sealed unto the day of redemption (Ephesians 4:30).

And be not drunk with wine, wherein is excess; but be filled with the Spirit (Ephesians 5:18).

If ye then be risen with Christ, seek those things which are above, where Christ sitteth on the right hand of God (Colossians 3:1).

This is a faithful saying, and worthy of all acceptation, that Christ Jesus came into the world to save sinners; of whom I am chief (I Timothy 1:15).

For this is good and acceptable in the sight of God our Saviour; who will have all men to be saved, and to come unto the knowledge of the truth (I Timothy 2:3-4).

. . . for I know whom I have believed, and am persuaded

that he is able to keep that which I have committed unto him against that day (II Timothy 1:12).

Not by works of righteousness which we have done, but according to his mercy he saved us, by the washing of regeneration, and renewing of the Holy Ghost (Titus 3:5).

How shall we escape, if we neglect so great salvation . . . (Hebrews 2:3).

. . . To day if ye will hear his voice, harden not your hearts, as in the provocation (Hebrews 3:15).

. . . To day, after so long a time; as it is said, To day if ye will hear his voice, harden not your hearts (Hebrews 4:7).

Let us therefore come boldly unto the throne of grace, that we may obtain mercy, and find grace to help in time of need (Hebrews 4:16).

Wherefore he is able also to save them to the uttermost that come unto God by him, seeing he ever liveth to make intercession for them (Hebrews 7:25).

And as it is appointed unto men once to die, but after this the judgment: so Christ was once offered to bear the sins of many; and unto them that look for him shall he appear the second time without sin unto salvation (Hebrews 9:27-28).

It is a fearful thing to fall into the hands of the living God (Hebrews 10:31).

But without faith it is impossible to please him: for he that cometh to God must believe that he is, and that he is a rewarder of them that diligently seek him (Hebrews 11:6).

Wherefore seeing we also are compassed about with so great a cloud of witnesses, let us lay aside every weight, and the sin which doth so easily beset us, and let us run with patience the race that is set before us, looking unto Jesus the author and finisher of our faith; who for the joy that was set before him endured the cross, despising the shame, and is set down at the right hand of the throne of God (Hebrews 12:1-2).

See that ye refuse not him that speaketh. For if they escaped not who refused him that spake on earth, much more shall not we escape, if we turn away from him that speaketh from heaven (Hebrews 12:25).

For our God is a consuming fire (Hebrews 12:29).

For whosoever shall keep the whole law, and yet offend in one point, he is guilty of all (James 2:10).

Ye adulterers and adulteresses, know ye not that the friendship of the world is enmity with God? whosoever therefore will be a friend of the world is the enemy of God (James 4:4).

Submit yourselves therefore to God. Resist the devil, and he will flee from you. Draw nigh to God, and he will draw nigh to you. Cleanse your hands, ye sinners; and purify your hearts, ye double minded (James 4:7-8).

Go to now, ye that say, To day or to morrow we will go into such a city, and continue there a year, and buy and sell, and get gain: whereas ye know not what shall be on the morrow. For what is your life? It is even a vapour, that appeareth for a little time, and then vanisheth away (James 4:13-14).

Therefore to him that knoweth to do good, and doeth it not, to him it is sin (James 4:17).

Brethren, if any of you do err from the truth, and one convert him; let him know, that he which converteth the sinner from the error of his way shall save a soul from death, and shall hide a multitude of sins (James 5:19-20).

For all flesh is as grass, and all the glory of man as the flower of grass. The grass withereth, and the flower thereof falleth away: but the word of the Lord endureth for ever. And this is the word which by the gospel is preached unto you (I Peter 1:24-25).

Who his own self bare our sins in his own body on the tree, that we, being dead to sins, should live unto righteousness: by whose stripes ye were healed (I Peter 2:24).

For Christ also hath once suffered for sins, the just for the unjust, that he might bring us to God, being put to death in the flesh, but quickened by the Spirit (I Peter 3:18).

For the time is come that judgment must begin at the house of God: and if it first begin at us, what shall the end be of them that obey not the gospel of God? And if the righteous scarcely be saved, where shall the ungodly and the sinner appear? (I Peter 4:17-18).

Wherefore the rather, brethren, give diligence to make your calling and election sure: for if ye do these things, ye shall never fall (II Peter 1:10).

The Lord is not slack concerning his promise, as some men count slackness; but is longsuffering to us-ward, not willing that any should perish, but that all should come to repentance (II Peter 3:9).

If we confess our sins, he is faithful and just to forgive us our sins, and to cleanse us from all unrighteousness (I John 1:9).

And he is the propitiation for our sins: and not for our's only, but also for the sins of the whole world (I John 2:2).

We know that we have passed from death unto life, because we love the brethren. He that loveth not his brother abideth in death (I John 3:14).

He that hath the Son hath the life; he that hath not the Son of God hath not the life (I John 5:12, A.S.V.).

These things have I written unto you that believe on the name of the Son of God; that ye may know that ye have eternal life . . . (I John 5:13).

Behold, he cometh with clouds; and every eye shall see him, and they also which pierced him: and all kindreds of the earth shall wail because of him. Even so, Amen (Revelation 1:7).

Remember therefore from whence thou art fallen, and repent, and do the first works; or else I will come unto thee quickly, and will remove thy candlestick out of his place, except thou repent (Revelation 2:5).

I know thy works, that thou art neither cold nor hot: I would thou wert cold or hot. So then because thou art lukewarm, and neither cold nor hot, I will spue thee out of my mouth (Revelation 3:15-16).

Behold, I stand at the door, and knock: if any man hear my voice, and open the door, I will come in to him, and will sup with him, and he with me (Revelation 3:20).

And said to the mountains and rocks, Fall on us, and hide us from the face of him that sitteth on the throne, and from the wrath of the Lamb: for the great day of his wrath is come; and who shall be able to stand? (Revelation 6:16-17).

And they overcame him by the blood of the Lamb, and by the word of their testimony; and they loved not their lives unto the death (Revelation 12:11).

And he saith unto me, Write, Blessed are they which are called unto the marriage supper of the Lamb . . . (Revelation 19:9).

Blessed and holy is he that hath part in the first resurrection: on such the second death hath no power, but they shall be priests of God and of Christ, and shall reign with him a thousand years (Revelation 20:6).

And I saw the dead, small and great, stand before God; and the books were opened: and another book was opened, which is the book of life: and the dead were judged out of those things which were written in the books, according to their works . . . And whosoever was not found written in the book of life was cast into the lake of fire (Revelation 20:12, 15).

But the fearful, and unbelieving, and the abominable, and murderers, and whoremongers, and sorcerers, and idolaters, and all liars, shall have their part in the lake which burneth with fire and brimstone: which is the second death (Revelation 21:8).

And the Spirit and the bride say, Come. And let him that heareth say, Come. And let him that is athirst come. And whosoever will, let him take the water of life freely (Revelation 22:17).

APPENDIX B

OTHER SOURCES OF INVITATION QUOTATIONS AND EXHORTATIONS

WHILE the Bible should be the principle source of quotations for evangelistic sermons and invitations, yet other sources may give us helpful material. These sources are too numerous and vast for us to explore here, but we can mention some of them.

In the great Gospel hymns, we have an almost inexhaustible fund of material for quotations. Next to the Scriptures, the Gospel hymns are best for quoting. They are familiar to people, have many sacred associations, are usually true to Scripture truth and the emotional element is prominent in them. A quotation from such hymns as "Just As I Am, Without One Plea," "Almost Persuaded" or "The Ninety and Nine" may wing its way into hearts with great effect.

The poets afford many apt quotations for invitational purposes. The best plan would be to file such quotations in a separate place, and use them when occasion demands. A poem often quoted is "The Doomed Man" by Joseph Addison Alexander. The first two stanzas reads as follows:

> There is a time, we know not when,
>   A point we know not where,
> That marks the destiny of men,
>   To glory or despair.

> There is a line, by us unseen,
>   That crosses every path,
> The hidden boundary between
>   God's patience and His wrath.

There are three other stanzas to this poem. Another such quotation is from James Russell Lowell's "The Present Crisis":

> Once to every man and nation
> Comes the moment to decide,
> In the strife of Truth with Falsehood,
> For the good or evil side.

Proverbs and slogans may occasionally furnish a good quotation, such as, "He who hesitates is lost," or

> Only one life for Jesus,
> 'Twill soon be past.
> Only what is done for Christ
> Will last.

As one hears or reads evangelistic sermons and appeals, he may often pick up valuable sentences or exhortations. From Dr. John W. Bradbury of New York City, editor of *The Watchman-Examiner*, the writer jotted down the following, as Dr. Bradbury was making his evangelistic appeal: "We march forward by decision"; and "New decision means new life."

All evangelistic preachers should guard against limiting themselves to a few quotations or exhortations, which become hackneyed and threadbare by constant use. Plenty of new and fresh material is available if we will look for and use it.

ADDITIONAL INVITATIONS

Dr. John R. Sampey's invitation. In *The Watchman-Examiner* for June 28, 1945, Dr. John R. Sampey, former president of the Southern Baptist Theological Seminary, published an article called "A Baptist Confessional." In this article Dr. Sampey tells how he learned to give an invitation at the close of each evangelistic service as broad as the Holy Spirit could wish. He invited people to come to the front during the invitation hymn and say to him (Dr. Sampey) whatever the Spirit prompted them to say. He particularly urged the need of confessing sins. He invited Christians and unsaved alike to come to him at the front and unburden their hearts in humble confession. He assured them that none would know what was being confessed except God, himself, and the confessor. He drew each person slightly aside while they confessed, so no one else could hear. Dr. Sampey says he has had as many as fifty and more lined up in the aisle waiting to speak to him; and that every sin in the catalogue except covetousness had been confessed to him. Through these confessions, he has been able to lead the unsaved to accept Christ as Saviour and Lord, and to direct Christians back to the path of cleansing, assurance and joy.

Dr. M. F. Ham's invitation. A good friend of the author went through a great evangelistic campaign with Evangelist M. F. Ham in Huntington, West Virginia, a number of years ago. During the first few weeks of the campaign, Dr. Ham hammered away at sin without giving any invitations. When conviction was deep, he began giving invitations and had some large responses. While the method of giving invitations varied, a characteristic invitation was to ask: "How many here are not saved, but you do not wish to die until you are saved? Put up your hands. You expect to be saved some day, even though you are not saved now, and you wish us to pray that God will let you live until you are saved. Put up your hands." Usually many hands went up, but the evangelist would plead for more hands for fifteen or twenty minutes while an invitation was being softly sung. After this, Dr. Ham would clear the front seats, and ask all who raised their hands to come to these seats. While they were seated, he would explain the way of salvation, illustrating and elaborating it very carefully and clearly, usually taking another ten or fifteen minutes. Then he would ask those at the front willing to accept Jesus Christ as Saviour and Lord right then to stand. If all did not stand, he would urge others to stand. Personal workers then would take the names, addresses, and church preferences of those who stood.

Youth for Christ invitations. While different kinds of invitations are used in these popular meetings, yet one used quite often in Chicago is as follows: The director has the audience bow in prayer, while he pleads earnestly and quietly for those concerned about their souls to raise their hands. Personal workers posted in various sections of the auditorium note the raised hands in their sections. After a prayer for those who have raised their hands, the director invites all such to come to the inquiry rooms. During the invitation hymn they come. If any do not come, personal workers go to them and personally invite them.

Dr. Chas. W. Koller's invitation. This well-known evangelistic preacher likes to remain at the front to greet inquirers while the pastor goes to the door to shake hands with the people as they leave. After a main invitation has been given, he says: "After the benediction I will remain at the front to meet any who may wish to talk with me about becoming Christians. The pastor will greet you at the door, but I will be here at the front to talk with you about the Christian life." Sometimes the unsaved will come alone, and at other times Christians will bring their unsaved friends and introduce them to the preacher.

Dr. Bob Jones' invitation. Dr. Bob Jones, Sr., gave an invitation in the Chicago Arena Campaign in which he first asked all the unsaved to raise their hands for prayer. He took some minutes to urge this response. Then an invitation hymn was sung during which those who had raised their hands were asked to come forward. Finally all the saved were asked to stand. This left the few remaining unsaved in the building still seated. He then pled with those remaining seated to stand and come forward to receive Christ. Some did. During this whole campaign not a large percentage of the audience was unsaved, but nearly all the unsaved responded to the invitation every night.

INDEX OF NAMES

(References are to pages)

SUBJECT INDEX

(References are to pages)